12582

PENGUIN BOOKS

BYZANTINE STYLE AND CIVILIZATION

Style and Civilization | Edited by John Fleming and Hugh Honour

Steven Runciman, second son of the 1st Viscount Runciman of Doxford was born in 1903 and was educated at Eton, where he was a King's Scholar, and at Trinity College, Cambridge. He was a Fellow of Trinity from 1927 to 1938 and lecturer at the University from 1932 to 1938.

In 1940 he became Press Attaché to the British Legation in Sofia, and he moved to the British Embassy in Cairo in 1941. From 1942 to 1945 he was Professor of Byzantine Art and History in the University of Istanbul, and then he served as a Representative of the British Council in Greece until 1947.

Sir Steven was Waynflete Lecturer at Magdalen College, Oxford, from 1953 to 1954, and has subsequently held many university appointments in Great Britain and America. He has been Chairman of the Anglo-Hellenic League and President of the British Institute of Archaeology at Ankara, and belongs to many learned societies.

Among his books are *Byzantine Civilization* (1933), *The Medieval Manichee* (1947), *The Sicilian Vespers* (1958), *The Fall of Constantinople, 1453* (1965), *The Great Church in Captivity* (1968), *The Orthodox Church and the Secular State* (1972), *The Byzantine Theocracy* (1977), *Mistra* (1980) and *A Traveller's Alphabet* (1991). His three-volume *History of the Crusades* (1951–4) is also published in Penguin. He was knighted in 1958.

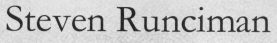

Steven Runciman

Byzantine
Style and Civilization

Penguin Books

PENGUIN BOOKS

Published by the Penguin Group
Penguin Books Ltd, 27 Wrights Lane, London W8 5TZ, England
Penguin Books USA Inc., 375 Hudson Street, New York, New York 10014, USA
Penguin Books Australia Ltd, Ringwood, Victoria, Australia
Penguin Books Canada Ltd, 10 Alcorn Avenue, Toronto, Ontario, Canada M4V 3B2
Penguin Books (NZ) Ltd, 182–190 Wairau Road, Auckland 10, New Zealand

Penguin Books Ltd, Registered Offices: Harmondsworth, Middlesex, England

First published in Pelican Books 1975
Reprinted in Penguin Books 1990
10 9 8 7 6 5 4 3 2

Printed in England by Clays Ltd, St Ives plc
Set in Monophoto Garamond

Designed by Gerald Cinamon and Paul McAlinden

Editorial Foreword

The series to which this book belongs is devoted to both the history and the problems of style in European art. It is expository rather than critical. The aim is to discuss each important style in relation to contemporary shifts in emphasis and direction both in the other, non-visual arts and in thought and civilization as a whole. By examining artistic styles in this wider context it is hoped that closer definitions and a deeper understanding of their fundamental character and motivation will be reached.

The series is intended for the general reader but it is written at a level which should interest the specialist as well. Beyond this there has been no attempt at uniformity. Each author has had complete liberty in his mode of treatment and has been free to be as selective as he wished – for selection and compression are inevitable in a series such as this, whose scope extends beyond the history of art. Not all great artists or great works of art can be mentioned, far less discussed. Nor, more specifically, is it intended to provide anything in the nature of an historical survey, period by period, but rather a discussion of the artistic concepts dominant in each successive period. And, for this purpose, the detailed analysis of a few carefully chosen issues is more revealing than the bird's-eye view.

Preface

In this book I have attempted to describe the conceptions that lay behind the art which emanated from Constantinople during the eleven centuries when that great city was the seat of the Christian Emperors of the East. Byzantine civilization is often dismissed as having been over-static. This is unjust; for no Empire can last for so long without movement. But it is true that the basic notion of the Empire remained the same. It was the Kingdom of God on earth, the pale reflection of the Kingdom of God in Heaven, earthbound because of its sins, but always with an Ideal that it should try to imitate. Its art was part of the pattern. The duty of art was to supplement the doctrine of the Incarnation, to show the divine in its light and colour in forms that human sensibility could comprehend. Inevitably its expression varied down the centuries. Techniques were improved. Fashions came and went. Classical memories jostled against memories from further to the East. But, whether lay or ecclesiastical, it remained a religious art; and its purpose gave it a unity that enables us to treat it as a whole.

It would take too long to mention all the works on Byzantine art which have helped me in this study; but I would like to record my special indebtedness to Father Gervase Mathew, whose *Byzantine Aesthetics* I have found to be a most valuable and stimulating guide. I owe much, too, to Professor André Grabar's works on Christian Iconography and on the Emperor in Byzantine art.

My thanks are due to Mr John Fleming and to Mr Hugh Honour, the editors of this series, and to the staff of Penguin Books. My acknowledgements to the institutions and publishers who have been good enough to supply photographs for the book are listed in the catalogue of illustrations. But I must mention my special gratitude to Professor V. N. Lazarev, of the Academy of Sciences of the USSR, for having sent me photographs of frescoes at Staraya Ladoga, Arkazhy and Vladimir, and to Professor Angelov, of the Bulgarian Academy, for having procured me photographs of the frescoes at Boiana.

S.R.

Byzantine
Style and Civilization

I

The Triumph of the Cross

I

It is given to very few men to be able to alter the whole course
of civilization. Constantine, surnamed the Great, had few of
the attributes of greatness. He lacked high intellectual stature;
his personality was not impressively dynamic; his vision was
limited. He was a soldier, a soldier's son, indifferently educated,
but gifted with a sound common-sense and a realization of
what was practical in warfare and in politics, a shrewd judge of
men. He was without mercy, humour or charm; but he had a
stern moral integrity. His father, an Illyrian soldier of un-
distinguished birth, had risen, by similar qualities and a touch
of good luck, to share the Imperial power. It was not an
unmixed advantage to be the son of an Emperor in the early
fourth century A.D. But Constantine made prudent use of his
assets. In 305, on his father's death, his army proclaimed him
Emperor. For some years he shared the Imperium uneasily
with partners, but from 324 to 337 he sat alone and supreme on
the Imperial throne.

The achievements that earned Constantine his surname were
three; and they gave to the Roman Empire a new pattern that
lasted, often modified but never wholly altered, for eleven
centuries. The empire over which he reigned had been through
a difficult period in the previous century. The age of the
Antonines, with its spurious atmosphere of bourgeois stability,
had come to a pitiful end, to be followed by uncertainty and
chaos. Economically, administratively, socially and morally,
the Roman world began to flounder through an era of transition. The system that shared the government of the provinces
between the Senate and the Imperator could no longer operate,
and no other system had yet been evolved that would suit both
the great urban centres of the East and the agricultural and
pastoral provinces of the West. The sprawling city of Rome,
with its senatorial traditions and its huge under-employed
proletariat, was no longer suitable as an administrative centre.

1. Constantine the Great. *c.* 312

Overtaxation, incessant civil war and the anomalies of slave labour helped to prevent any economic or social stability. Barbarian tribes, as they began to learn the techniques of civilization, pressed from over the frontier, longing to join in the amenities of the Empire. To contain them and to provide some sort of police force within the Empire, a huge army was essential and commanded the only positive power, but the army seldom acted as a unit. Individual regiments produced candidates for the Imperial throne, and the decision was reached by warfare. The soldiers themselves were increasingly recruited from barbarian tribes who lacked the old Roman belief in *gravitas* and civil responsibility. Culturally there had always been a division between the two halves of the Empire, the Greek-speaking East with its long traditions of civilization and the Latin-speaking West, whose civilization came for the most part from a comparatively recent Roman conquest. There was no one religious force strong enough to impose moral unity on the Empire. The old gods had been local or tribal; and the attempt to give the Roman pantheon a universal status by a wholesale identification of its members with provincial deities failed, largely because no one believed any longer in the Roman gods. The city of Rome might be proclaimed as a presiding genius; but the city was no longer the effective seat of government. Even less convincing was the attribution of divinity to the Emperor. The characters and the unpleasant fate of most of the Emperors scarcely suggested that they were divine. Moreover the notion was challenged by the growing desire of men and women of the time for a religion that would be both universal and genuinely spiritual; but no such religion had as yet made good its claim.

Constantine's main reforms had been foreshadowed a few decades earlier by the Emperor Diocletian. He had tried to solve the economic problem by freezing prices and wages and forcing men to follow their fathers' professions. But the system was too rigid and could not succeed while the currency varied in true value from place to place and from time to time. He had tried to establish a competent civil service owing everything to the Emperor, and to divide the Empire into local regions or 'dioceses', each with a fixed capital, under a tetrarchy of two co-equal Emperors, each with a Caesar under him. But the Tetrarchy took no account of human ambitions and rivalries. Ensuing civil wars kept the monarchs continually on the move; and the new capitals were neglected. He tried to give moral unity to the Empire by enhancing the divinity of the Emperor. He developed Court ceremonial. The secretariat that accompanied him was known as the Sacred Company. New religious sects who refused to pay formal homage to his divinity were subject to persecution. But though Diocletian himself survived to enjoy a few years of luxurious retirement, the Emperors remained unconvincing gods, and the persecuted sects grew stronger through suffering. As the Christian Tertullian had noted a century earlier, 'the blood of the martyrs is the seed of the Church'.

Constantine was more prudent and more practical. Of his three great achievements the first, though it might be the most interesting to modern statesmen, is the least well documented. Somehow he succeeded in giving stability to the currency, by calling in bad money and by establishing a restricted number of Imperial mints whose gold coins had a fixed relationship to his gold standard, the nugget known as the solidus [2]. For seven centuries this gold standard was maintained, making the Imperial city the financial centre of the world.

2. Gold solidus of Constantine the Great

Constantine's second achievement was to found a new Imperial city. He saw that if an effective civil service was to exist there must be a fixed seat of government. Rome itself, with its old senatorial traditions, its unruly mob, and its vulnerability caused by the need to import all its food from overseas, was no longer a suitable administrative capital. After some hesitation he picked for its site the Greek city of

Byzantium, on the extreme tip of Europe, where the narrow strait of the Bosphorus opens out into the Sea of Marmara. It was a superb site, on a peninsula that was roughly triangular, with curved sides, the convex side protected by the sea and the concave by the magnificent harbour of the Golden Horn. Its landward side was comparatively short and easy to fortify. It commanded the sea route from the Black Sea to the Mediterranean and the easiest land route from Europe into Western Asia. It was well placed for the two frontiers that were of most concern to the Empire, the Danube frontier beyond which lived the most restless of the barbarians, and the Eastern frontier beyond which was the active, aggressive Kingdom of Sassanid Persia. Its only disadvantage was its climate, damp and often grey, with an icy wind blowing all winter from the Russian Steppes, down the channel of the Bosphorus, and in summer all too often a sultry wind from the south, even more enervating in its effect. This city was to be New Rome, but to most of the world it was known as Constantinople after its founder, while the Greeks who lived there called it just the City, '*stan polin*' in their local accent: whence comes the modern name of Istanbul.

Thirdly Constantine altered the whole spiritual life of the future by giving official recognition to the Christian Church. His own conversion was probably genuine, though he never lost his taste for the cult of the Undying Sun. But the recognition was wise, both for its immediate and its long-term effects. Of the universal religions that were seeking to displace the outworn pagan gods, the Mystery Cults of Isis and of the Great Mother were concentrated at a few centres and too esoteric to be accepted by the masses. Mithraism, the cult of the Undying Sun, was the army's favourite religion, but it had little appeal to laymen and none at all to women. Neoplatonism was more of a philosophy than a religion and was unintelligible to the less well educated. Christianity, with its doctrine of the equality of each individual soul, had a universal appeal, to rich and poor, to women and to slaves. It was well organized. The churches throughout the Empire, though they might bicker, were in close touch with each other; and persecution had proved to them the need for solidarity. Their charity towards their needier members was efficient and impressive. Moreover, at least since the days of Justin Martyr and Clement of Alexandria in the second century A.D., the Church had included many of the best intellects of the time who could express the faith in terms acceptable to thinkers brought up on Greek philosophy. At the time of Constantine's conversion admitted Christians probably numbered only about a seventh of the Empire's population. But their influence spread far wider. By allying himself with them Constantine won the support of the strongest individual group in the Roman world of the time; and Imperial patronage gave the Christians such encouragement that by the end of the fourth century they easily dominated the Empire.

These three achievements of Constantine formed the foundations on which the civilization that we call Byzantine was built. Their effect was not immediate. It was some time before Constantinople became the exclusive residence of the Emperors. It was some time before the new wealth engendered by Constantine's monetary reforms was effective. It was some time before the Emperors learnt how to make full use of the Church, and the Church full use of the Emperors. But by the end of the fourth century the Emperor was the holy Emperor, living in the Sacred Palace surrounded by liturgical ceremony, and, so long as he were worthy, revered as the Viceroy of God; and the Emperor in his turn was devoting energy and riches to the glory and welfare of the Christian Church. Byzantine civilization was to undergo many modifications down the centuries; but its bases remained constant; and this is true of its noblest form of expression, its art.

II

The earliest Christians took little interest in art. They were largely influenced by the Stoics, to whom art was irrelevant, and they were under the shadow of Mosaic Law, with its stern ban on idols and graven images. In any case, a poor and often persecuted community cannot afford ostentation. To decorate the meeting-houses used by the Christians would have been expensive and would have drawn unwelcome attention to them. But the human desire for decoration is profound, and the human desire to wear a distinctive badge is widespread. So, while the early Church Fathers such as Clement of Alexandria and Tertullian firmly forbade anything that might be considered to be an image, Clement allowed that Christians might wear signet-rings on which were carved objects such as

3. Fish and Basket. *c.* 250.
Wall-painting in Catacomb of Saint Callixtus, Rome

a dove, a ship, a fish or a lyre, each of them a symbol of the
Christian life but none of them necessarily revealing the wearer
to be a Christian.

Symbols were theologically permissible and politically safe;
and the taste for them grew. The phoenix rising from its ashes
signified the rebirth of the soul after purification. The peacock
drinking at the fountain was the incorruptible soul attaining
immortality at the Fountain of Life [4, 5]. The lamb was the
Lamb of God. Soon these harmless birds and beasts were
joined by figures, by a lady gloriously attired whom pagans
might mistake for an empress or a goddess but who was in
truth the Church, or a good shepherd, whom the pagan world
knew as a symbol of philanthropy or might believe to be
Orpheus, but who was Christ himself [6, 7]. From there it was
an easy step, as the Christians grew more self-confident, to
want to have representations of Christ and his Mother and the
Saints. The Emperor Alexander Severus (222–35), who was
oecumenically minded, was said by a later and unreliable source
to have had in his oratory statues of Orpheus, Moses, Christ

4. Sarcophagus of Archbishop Theodore of Ravenna.
Sixth century

5. Peacock capital. *c.* 540. Constantinople

6. (*below left*). The Good Shepherd. *c.* 260. Catacomb of Saint Callixtus, Rome

7. The Good Shepherd. *c.* 300

and Apollonius of Tyana. Legends are usually based on fact; and the tale suggests that such images were obtainable at the time. By the following century portraits of Christ were on sale in Palestine. Constantine's sister Constantia asked Bishop Eusebius of Caesarea to procure one for her. But Eusebius, who belonged to the old school, refused and rebuked her sharply for her idolatry.

By that time the walls of most Christian meeting-houses were covered with painted decoration, and the painters were beginning to depict Christ and the Saints. The chief repositories of this art were the Roman catacombs, the underground chambers in which Christians were buried. Many of the

8. The Children in the Fiery Furnace. Early fourth century. Catacomb of Priscilla, Rome

catacomb paintings belong to a later date, when the chambers had become acknowledged shrines. But the surviving older fragments show that the art was in the traditional pictorial style of the Greco-Roman world, akin to the earlier but more sophisticated paintings at Pompeii [8]. In the provinces, especially in the East, there was a strong Jewish influence. The paintings in the little chapel at Dura on the Euphrates clearly owe a great deal to the paintings in the large near-by synagogue, whose rich congregation considered that the Mosaic ban did not apply to pictorial art [9, 10].

9. The Ark at Rest in the Temple. Early third century.
From the synagogue at Dura

This humble, popular and rather old-fashioned art was suited to a sect that was still subject to persecution and one whose leaders were not at all sure that they approved of art in any form. It was completely unsuitable when Christianity received the blessing of the Emperor and became the ruling religion in the Empire.

The open profession of Christianity and the rapidly increasing number of Christians demanded at once the building of new and larger places of worship. The older type of temple could not be used. It had been intended to be admired from without. The interior had been reserved for the deity, not for the rites of a congregation. Moreover, temples were tainted;

22

10. David anointed by Samuel. Early third century.
From the synagogue at Dura

they were shrines of idolatry. Theodosius I in the late fourth century ordered that temples of outstanding beauty should be preserved; but public opinion did not support him. Many temples were left to fall into ruins. Others were pulled to pieces by fanatical Christian mobs. Others were more carefully dismembered, often on Imperial orders, so that their columns and marble slabs and panels could be used in new churches. A few, such as the Parthenon at Athens, survived through being adapted for the new religion. But that meant the replanning of the interior and was seldom successful.

The type of building most suitable for adaptation was the basilica, the rectangular public assembly-room and law-court. It had its entrance door on one of the longer sides, and the apse containing the magistrate's seat opposite. The Christians moved the door to one of the shorter sides, with the apse, in which the altar was placed, opposite, preferably at the eastern end. The space in front of the apse was reserved for the celebration of the rites. Colonnades down each of the longer sides helped to support the roof or, alternatively, a gallery which in turn supported the roof. There thus were side aisles or galleries which could be reserved for women in parts of the world where it was thought unseemly for the sexes to mingle at worship. The central space was kept unencumbered for the bulk of the congregation.

The great rotundas of the Roman world, circular buildings covered with a dome, could also be adapted; for they too provided the necessary open floor space. They could also be copied on a smaller scale to serve as martyria, to house the body and the relics of a saint, or as baptisteries; for baptism was not yet the perfunctory affair that it later became in the West.

All these new buildings required new forms of decoration. Statuary in the round was out of place in a building where the emphasis was on the interior and the interior had to be kept free of obstructions. A statue would have to be placed in a niche in the wall, where only the frontal view was of importance; or, better, carving should be in bas-relief. The consequent decline of free statuary was due more to its unsuitability than to the Mosaic ban. It was at a later date that it was discouraged on theological grounds. In the sixth century the pious Emperor Justinian did not hesitate to erect statues of himself and his Empress Theodora in public squares and gardens. In church buildings the important task now was to decorate the walls themselves. Fresco-painters were called in, to produce something grander than the decoration that had sufficed for small meeting-houses and catacombs. But soon their work was superseded, when funds allowed, by a new branch of art which answered far better to the requirements of the time.

Floor-mosaics had long been known to the Roman world. Pavements had been made with patterns or pictures composed out of small cubes of variously coloured stones or marbles. The work was often of the greatest delicacy [11, 12]. But the stone cube is heavy. Attempts to use it for wall mosaics were

11. The Good Shepherd. Late fifth century. Aquileia

12 (*opposite*). Fishing scene. Late fifth century. Aquileia

unsuccessful. Then it was discovered, probably first in Alexandria with its vast glass-factories, that glass cubes were far more suitable for fixing on walls. They were lighter in weight and they were more luminous. The glass could be dyed, or coated with gold or silver dust. It could be cut rough or smooth. It could be set at the angle best fitted to catch the light. Patterns and pictorial scenes in mosaic could now be placed on the walls, and by careful lighting they seemed not to enclose but to enlarge the space that they surrounded.

At first, as was inevitable, decorators were not always adept in handling the new medium. The late fourth-century mosaic vaulting in Santa Costanza in Rome is copied from a floor mosaic and looks rather as if someone had tried to fix a carpet on the ceiling [13, 14]. The great Roman basilica known later as Santa Maria Maggiore, dating from the early fifth century, has mosaics of excellent quality so placed, high above the

13. Traditio Legis.
Late fourth century. S. Costanza, Rome

14 (*opposite*). S. Costanza, Rome. Late fourth century

15. S. Maria Maggiore, Rome. 432-40

16. The Presentation.
Mid fifth century. S. Maria Maggiore, Rome

colonnade, that it is quite impossible to see them properly [15, 16]. The designs were doubtless ordered from some workshop without any thought of their future setting. The still more sophisticated mosaics in the curves of the rotunda of

17. Saints Onesiphorus and Porphyrius.
Late fourth century. Thessalonica

Saint George at Thessalonica, a little later in date, seem to have
been designed for a flat surface [17].

It was in smaller buildings, in martyria and baptisteries, that
the mosaicists learnt to perfect their art. The more intimate
proportions were better suited to decorative experiments. Of
the buildings that survive, it is in the so-called Mausoleum of
Galla Placidia at Ravenna, dating from the middle of the fifth
century, that we first find mosaic decoration in complete
harmony with the architecture [18, 19]. The technique was not
yet as delicate as it was to become in later centuries, when there
was greater ingenuity in varying the size, the material and the
setting of the cubes. But the general effect is superb.

18. Mausoleum of Galla Placidia, Ravenna. *c.* 425

The floor mosaic continued to be made, with the old technique and in the old style, for a long time to come, especially in secular buildings. It reached its culmination in the floors of the Great Palace at Constantinople, which some scholars have dated as late as the second half of the sixth century.[1] But fashion was changing. More simply patterned marble floors were preferred, and carpets came into use. Indeed, if walls were decorated pictorially, it would be excessive to have pictorial floors as well.

The new status of Christianity enabled the subject-matter of Christian art to be broadened. The graven image, or, at least, the painted image, had come to stay. In the late fourth century that stern opponent of heresy, Epiphanius of Salamis, tore down a curtain in a church at Caesarea because there was depicted on it a portrait of Christ. But his cause was lost, at least until the eighth century, when it temporarily triumphed under the Iconoclastic Emperors. Not only did portraits of Christ and the Mother of God multiply, but also pictorial scenes of episodes in the Bible story. These scenes were never merely the 'poor man's Bible', as they became in the West. They were, indeed, useful as didactic illustrations; but each of them contained a deeper significance on which the initiate could ponder. Symbols, which to Clement of Alexandria had merely been prudently disguised tokens of the Faith, increased in number and took on a fuller meaning. Dolphins, vines and anchors proliferated. If Old Testament scenes were depicted they now carried a second message. Adam and Eve were the forerunners of Christ and his Church. Jonah descending into the whale's belly foreshadowed Christ's descent into Hell [22]. Abraham entertaining the three angels at Mamre bore witness to the Holy Trinity and carried a further significance as the Communion Feast. New Testament scenes, too, could be given a double interpretation. The woman of Samaria was the Church waiting to draw from the well the waters of immortality. The raising of Lazarus is Christ's own conquest of death. Later Church Fathers, while they approved of the symbolic interpretation of holy scenes, began to find the single symbolic object irrelevant. The Council *in Trullo*, meeting in Constantinople in 691, tried to ban its use. It failed. Throughout the

1. See below, pp. 73, 217.

20 (*opposite*). Wooden door, S. Sabina, Rome. 422–40

21 (*left*). The Ascension of Elijah.
Detail from the door of S. Sabina,
Rome

22. A philosopher between Jonah
and Orant and the Good Shepherd.
Detail of a sarcophagus.
Probably late third century

23. The Good Shepherd between two rams.
Detail of a sarcophagus. Fourth century

Byzantine centuries peacocks continued to drink from the
Fountain of Life, dolphins to battle in the ocean of eternity,
the True Vine to spread its tendrils, and stars to glimmer on
the ceilings as gems in the robe of the Church herself, the
Woman of the Apocalypse.

III

These developments in technique and in subject-matter were
in the spirit of the time. The Triumph of the Cross under
Constantine brought into Christian art circles patrons in touch
with the latest cultural fashions. The most formidable intellectual opponents of Christianity had been the Neoplatonists,
headed by Plotinus, who seems to have had little interest in the
new religion, and his successors, Porphyry, who wrote against
the Christians, and, later, Proclus, who was fiercely hostile to
them. It is ironical that the Christian victory should have led to
the victory of Neoplatonic theories of art. It was the price that
Christianity paid for becoming the fashionable religion.

To the Classical world beauty was to be seen in the balanced
proportion of parts and the theory of tones. Art should be, so
to speak, an improved version of nature with the discords
eliminated. The theory of art was somewhat pedestrian.
According to Aristotle, 'the reason why people enjoy pictures
is because the spectator learns and infers what each object
is . . . and, if he has not seen the object before, the pleasure is
produced not by the imitation but by the execution, the colour,
or some such cause'. Plato had been a little more imaginative
in his view; but he thought art dangerous because of its

36

possible emotional effect, disliking it for almost the same reasons as those for which his Neoplatonic successors approved of it. To Plotinus the value of the emotion engendered by art lies in the comprehension that beauty is not concerned with material forms but with eternal concepts. 'Beauty', he says, 'is that which irradiates symmetry rather than symmetry itself.' The form, he points out, exists in the artist's mind before he executes the work of art. The arts do not exist to reproduce nature but to go back to the ideas from which nature itself is derived. The material thing, he explains, becomes beautiful by communicating the thought which comes from the divine. That is to say, the artist should not be concerned with copying nature but with interpreting ideas. The bonds of a naturalistic technique are no longer relevant. As a result the individual work of art begins to be downgraded. Art has no business to concern itself with individual objects; its products should be parts of a universal whole. The artist too begins to lose his individual identity. He becomes instead one of a team of interpreters of the divine. That is why we know the names of so few Byzantine artists.

In other ways, too, Plotinus foreshadowed later taste. He was obsessed by light. 'Beauty of colour', he says, 'derives from the conquest of the darkness inborn in matter by the pouring-in of light, the unembodied.' The Byzantines agreed with this. They held light, the first-created element, in supreme regard. They were fascinated by its varying effects, and, like Plotinus, they equated colour with the intensities of light. Like him, also, they found the light of the flame almost more exciting than the light of the sun. 'Fire', says Plotinus, 'is splendid beyond all material things . . . and gives the form of colour from the splendour of its light.' The flickering, lively quality of flame was particularly pleasing to Byzantine taste. It was this interest in light that made the mosaic the perfect medium for Byzantine art, as the churches of the sixth and later centuries were to show.

Already in the third century Neoplatonic ideas became apparent in Roman Imperial art, particularly in Imperial portrait sculpture. Hitherto Imperial portraits had been essentially portraits, though, like all official portraits, they emphasized the more estimable characteristics of the sitter. A change came about the time of the Emperor Gallienus (253–68). He was a Roman of the old school, but on his coins he identified himself with gods, with Hercules or Mercury, or with the genius of Rome [24]. He is an Imperial divinity rather than an Emperor. As with many later Imperial portraits, his eyes look upwards, to receive grace from heaven. Henceforward there was a growing desire to give an impression of majesty and power rather than to dwell upon individual traits. The portraits are portraits still, but simplified. The various statues of Constantine the Great show his features recognizably, but they might also be illustrations of the concept of authority. The idea is becoming more important than the earthly material.

24. Gold coin of the Emperor Gallienus

25. Theodosius I and his sons receiving gifts from the barbarians. Detail from the base for an Egyptian obelisk in Constantinople. c. 390

Conversion to Christianity did not lessen the Imperial authority but, rather, gave it divine sanction. Statues in this style continued to be made until the early seventh century. But with the decline in free statuary there was a growing taste for Imperial art on a smaller scale, for ivory or metal-work with bas-relief carving, which, whatever its size, still managed to emphasize Imperial majesty. On such pieces facial expression could not be effectively shown. So, if the Emperor is depicted with attendants, he is far larger than they are, as on the silver dish of Theodosius I, now in Madrid [26, 27, 28]. On ivory

26. Theodosius I and his sons, with allegorical figures.
Silver missorium. 488

27 and 28. Details from 26

29. Mounted Emperor, probably Justinian I. *c.* 530

diptychs the Emperor or Consul is unnecessarily big. On the Barberini ivory, now in the Louvre, Justinian is disproportionate in size even to his horse, and for the whole design [29]. Even in the sixth-century mosaics in San Vitale at Ravenna the Empress Theodora, notoriously a tiny woman, is taller than any of her Court [30].

The Triumph of the Cross meant the triumph of these new ideas and new techniques designed to satisfy the spiritual and practical needs of the triumphant Church and of an Empire that was now the earthly image of the Kingdom of Heaven. It did not bring an immediate revolution in art. Older fashions

30. The Empress Theodora and her court. *c.* 547

31. Old and New Testament scenes on a reliquary casket. *c.* 370

32. Bridal casket of Secundus and Projecta. Late fourth century

persisted. In purely secular art the classical tradition continued
with little change for many centuries to come [32]. Much of the
new work was experimental and unsatisfactory. The later
fourth and the fifth centuries were troubled times. Paganism
was still formidable. The civil service was mainly manned by
pagans. The School of Athens, led by thinkers such as Proclus,
was far from being a spent force. The Church itself was rent by
great Christological controversies. The army was filled with
barbarians belonging mainly to the Arian heresy. Art could not
but reflect the unsettled atmosphere of the times. It was
inconsistent and unsure of itself. A few buildings such as the
Mausoleum of Galla Placidia gave an indication that a new
style was emerging. But it is not until the sixth century that we
can really say that Byzantine art had arrived.

2

The Sixth-century Synthesis

I

By the beginning of the sixth century the western provinces of the old Roman Empire were almost entirely in the hands of barbarians. Rome itself had twice been sacked, by the Visigoths and by the Vandals. The historic Eastern provinces of Egypt and Syria were torn by heretical movements. Across the Eastern frontier Sassanid Persia was a perpetual menace, and new barbarian tribes were pressing on the Danube frontier. But the reforms of Constantine had justified themselves. Despite the expenses of government and the extravagance of individual Emperors the Empire was rich, owing above all to the reliability of its currency. Even in lands as far away as Ceylon merchants demanded to be paid in the Imperial coinage. Constantinople, which at first had been one capital added to many others, was now the sole residence of the Emperors, who saw the strategic and economic value of its site. The civil service was centred there and growing in power; and round the Palace there were springing up the most up-to-date factories and workshops. It was to Constantinople that every young man of ambition, whatever his craft or trade, came to seek his fortune. The older metropoles, Alexandria and Antioch, were losing ground in comparison.

The Emperor now was the sole Christian Emperor, the unquestioned head of the Christian commonwealth. His colleagues in the West had been suppressed by barbarian chieftains who preferred that their Roman subjects should acknowledge a distant suzerain rather than one at hand. He still had to deal with heresy and with the last traces of paganism. But at Constantinople he could surround himself with the pomp and ceremony that befitted the supreme magistrate of Christendom, the figure who represented God before the people and the people before God. He was the Sacred Emperor, and the palace in which he lived was the Sacred Palace. The governance of the Christian Empire was a holy task, and the ceremonies with which it was organized and expressed were becoming religious ceremonies, almost as sacred as the celebration of the Mysteries in the churches. A coronation ceremony was now needed; and from 450 onwards this was performed by the senior bishop of the Empire, the Patriarch of Constantinople; and in it the Emperor was endowed with some of the attributes of priesthood. His autocracy was limited. If he was considered by the Church authorities to be heretical, or grossly immoral, the Patriarch might withhold coronation until he promised to reform. If from harsh tyranny or hopeless folly he alienated the populace, his sacrosanctity did not protect him from riots that might lead to his deposition or even his death. God's viceroy must be worthy of the viceroyalty. It was unwise for him to lose the support of the army. But still more important to him was the loyalty of the civil service, centred round the Palace, a body of devoted men chosen for their intellectual ability, who controlled the central administration and the purse-strings of the Empire. If they found the Emperor inadequate, they had their own methods for disposing of him.

This great Christian Empire had need of an art that would enhance and give deeper meaning to its majesty and its sanctity. Unfortunately it is impossible to trace the early development of this Constantinopolitan art. Apart from the Theodosian walls and the Hippodrome and a few columns, there is no building standing in Constantinople that dates from before the sixth century. There is no illustrated manuscript of the first order that we can safely date before the same period. In the provinces buildings and artifacts seem to have followed local traditions, with a few modern features added, such as the mosaics that fit so oddly in the Roman basilicas and rotundas. These provincial schools were not static. Within the cultural sphere of Antioch architectural experiments were made, notably in the churches of southern Asia Minor [33, 34]; and artists born in the provinces brought these new fashions with them to Constantinople. But art was still unofficial and some-what sporadic. The first Christian potentates, Constantine, his mother Helena and his son Constantius, seem to have built churches as acts of individual piety. Rich individual patrons still existed in the fifth century. In the early sixth century we find churches built at Constantinople by the Lady Juliana Anicia, a millionairess who from her descent from Theodosius I

33. Saint Symeon (Qalat Siman) in Northern Syria.
Late fifth century

34. Saint Symeon (Qalat Siman) in Northern Syria.
Late fifth century

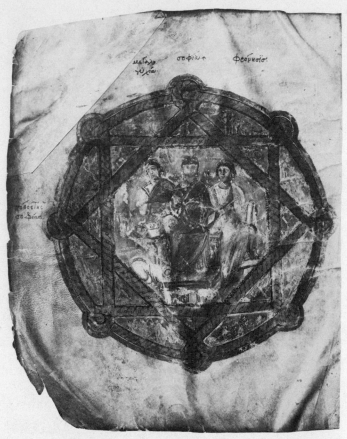

35. Princess Juliana Anicia. 512

could afford to despise the upstart Imperial line [35]. Her
great church of Saint Polyeuct, whose foundations are now
being excavated, may explain to us much of the technical
development of Constantinopolitan art. But it was the last
important edifice there to owe its origin to a private patron for
some eight centuries. Henceforward churches, manuscripts,
ivories and other works of importance were commissioned by
the Emperor or members of his family, who could call upon
the resources of the Imperial workshops and craftsmen; and
the bills would be paid by a civil servant, the Count of the
Sacred Largesse. In the provinces monks might use local talent

to paint their church walls and local magnates might use local craftsmen to ornament their country houses. But there is all the difference in the world between, say, the Cappadocian rock chapels of the early eleventh century and the contemporary mosaics of the Church of the Nea Moni at Chios, specially commissioned by the Emperor.

II

The Emperor responsible for the new order was Justinian I (527-65). His uncle and predecessor, Justin I, was an Illyrian peasant in origin. But Justinian himself had received a fair education, and he was married to a wife, the actress Theodora, who, however disreputable her early career may have been, had an intelligence and a forcefulness far acuter than his own. It was her courage that had saved his throne at the time of the rebellion known as the Nika riots. Justinian was determined, whatever the cost, to reoccupy effectively the western provinces ruled by the barbarians: in which he was only partially and temporarily successful. He sought, in vain, to restore religious unity throughout the Empire, even though Theodora while she lived pursued a different religious policy. He inspired his legal advisers to codify Roman Law, introducing Christian principles. And he was determined that the Imperial City should be worthy of Imperial majesty, and that provincial capitals and holy sites should receive their proper share of patronage. Like many other autocrats he believed that great buildings were a proper expression of greatness.

In Constantinople the devastation caused by the Nika riots gave Justinian his opportunity. Of the two great churches of the city, Saint Sophia, the Church of the Holy Wisdom of God founded by Constantine and Constantius and already extensively rebuilt after earthquake damage, had been burned beyond repair. The Church of the Holy Apostles, where Constantine lay in his sarcophagus, was in almost equal need of reconstruction. Moreover the city, with its growing population and the elimination of paganism, required many more Church buildings. After the reconquest of Italy it was proper that the capital of the province, Ravenna, should have its share of buildings, for which the money and designs would have to be provided from Constantinople. There were shrines that needed repair in Jerusalem and on Sinai. In addition, more halls were needed for the Sacred Palace, and all over the

Empire public buildings and castles were required. The historian Procopius' list of the Emperor's buildings omits those in Italy and Greece but includes several hundred items.

So vast a programme allowed for experiments. But the experiments were confident, and they were based on the conception that a building with all its decoration and fittings must be designed as a whole with its purpose firmly in mind. There was to be no more timorous toying with wooden domes. The domes must be part of the structure. Mosaic designs were no longer to be taken from picture-books regardless of the siting of the wall that they had to beautify. They must be designed so as to give the right impression in their ultimate destination. The Romans seem to have achieved their triumphs of engineering as a result of practical empirical experience. The Greeks enjoyed theory, and they were fascinated by mathematics, especially by geometry. When Justinian wanted an architect for Saint Sophia he chose a leading geometrician, Anthemius of Tralles, and, to assist him, another geometrician, Isidore of Miletus.

Anthemius is the only great Byzantine artist of whose life we know any details. He came from the professional classes. His father was a physician, as was one of his brothers, another being a surgeon, another a lawyer and the fourth a professor of rhetoric. It was as a professor of geometry that he made his name; and, to judge from his surviving writings, geometry, not architecture, remained his supreme passion. A vague phrase from the historian Agathias suggests that he had some knowledge of painting and sculpture, which doubtless strengthened his authority where the decoration of his buildings was concerned. But his task was, in the words of Agathias, to 'apply geometry to solid matter'. In Byzantine Greek wording he was a *mechanikos*, an engineer. The word 'architect' was given to the builders and masons who worked under him. Despite his renown he seems never to have become rich. He lived quietly in a small flat in Constantinople. Though he was the greatest Byzantine architect his career was probably typical of them all. They were professors and civil servants living unostentatiously in the cultivated circles that were the most solid element in Byzantine life.

The architecture of Saint Sophia is essentially an architecture of space. The Byzantines seem to have concerned themselves much less about the exterior aspect of their buildings: though we can now only guess at what the outward aspect of sixth-

36. Saint Sophia, Constantinople. 532-7

37. Saint Sophia, 532–7.
(The minarets have been removed on this photograph)

century Constantinople must have been. From the outside the mass of the great church rises not unharmoniously but not very gracefully. The huge buttresses added to support the dome some eight centuries after its construction and later buttressing may have distorted the original appearance; and the Turkish minarets, though they enrich the sky line, interfere with the proportions. It was the interior that was all-important. The aim there was not only to create space, needed for the cere-monies of the chief cathedral of the Empire, but also to create the feeling of still greater space. The technical problem was to fit a soaring dome on a huge rectangular, almost square, base. Saint Sophia is often said to be a domed basilica. Like the longer old basilicas it had side-aisles separated by pillars from the body of the church and carrying lateral galleries; but the dome imposed a centralization quite alien to the basilicas of the past. The transition from the rectangle to the circle from which the dome sprang was made by means of pendentives. Pen-dentives were not a new discovery but they had never been used on such a scale before; and the curving of their triangular surface allowed the eye to pass more easily from the rectangle to the circle than did the more usual device of the squinch. Similarly the four curved sides of the basket-capitals that surmounted most of the columns in the church were intended to ease the transition from the circular column to the rectangular superstructure.

The building of Saint Sophia was begun in 532, soon after the Nika riots, and completed in 535. Till modern times no other building contained so vast an open floor-space under a single roof. It would be inappropriate to discuss here all the technical devices by which the result was achieved. Our concern is the impression that it was intended to give and gave to contemporaries. To Procopius the semi-dome at the east end was 'admirable for its beauty but the cause of terror from the apparent weakness of its structure'. The dome, he thought, seemed not to rest upon a solid foundation but to cover the space as though it were suspended by a golden chain from heaven. The triumphant boldness of the architecture continued to impress visitors throughout the ages. But in fact Anthemius made some miscalculations. Twice, Procopius tells us, the Emperor had to intervene with practical suggestions. The dome itself was so delicately balanced that it came crashing down in an earthquake in 558. Isidore the younger, the nephew of Anthemius' colleague, had to rebuild it at a slightly steeper

38 (*below*). Saint Sophia, the main door

39. Saint Sophia, interior view

angle, and seems at the same time to have added the huge
external buttresses at the end of the lateral walls. This dome
was badly cracked in an earthquake some four centuries later
and was rebuilt, apparently on Isidore's pattern, by an
Armenian architect, Tirdaṭ of Ani. The eastern semi-dome had
to be repaired after another earthquake in 1346.

Anthemius as *mechanikos* was in charge of the decoration of
the building. Here the intention was to give an impression of

40. Saint Sophia, interior view

movement by covering the walls with shimmering colours. The
columns were of coloured marble or porphyry or basalt. Slabs
of similar colours covered the piers and the lower walls. The
upper walls, the ceiling of the vaults and dome were covered in
mosaic, mainly simple polychrome crosses or star-shaped
patterns on a gold ground. Cubes of semi-precious stones were
used to vary the effect of the glass. The capitals were mainly of
drilled basket-work. There were screens of marble bas-relief,
depicting flowers and birds and vines and ivy leaves. The great
ambo, or pulpit, was of ivory and silver, ornamented with
gold. It is doubtful whether Justinian's church contained
pictorial mosaics. Those described by Paulus Silentiarius in his

41. Saint Sophia, interior of dome

poem on the church were probably added during the younger Isidore's reconstruction. But there was certainly a huge silk hanging which Justinian donated, depicting Christ between St Peter and St Paul, with symbols of the Imperial Philanthropy around the borders.

The decoration owed much of its effect to a subtle use of light. The Byzantines were deeply interested in the study of geodesy, the measurement of surface and volume, and of optics, *Katoptika*, the relation of seen objects with the eye. Geodesy and optics were combined to influence the decoration of curved surfaces. But this involved effects of lighting. The windows in Saint Sophia were placed with careful calculation, the small windows round the base of the dome being especially effective. They were of clear glass. Elsewhere thin alabaster was used, to diffuse the light. In some churches, though probably not in Saint Sophia, lightly coloured glass was also employed. But many of the services of the church took place after dark; and the sky at Constantinople was often overcast. The decoration had to be related to the lamps and candles in the building: and indeed Byzantine mosaics are at their most effective when they are seen by the flickering light of flames. To secure this aim infinite pains were taken in the placing not only of the marbles but of every single mosaic cube. There were tiny but deliberate variations in the thickness of the plaster in which the cubes were fixed and in the angles at which each cube was set.

Saint Sophia thus illustrates the basic principles of Byzantine art. There must be symmetry, achieved by the perfect realization of geometrical possibilities. There must be a feeling of movement; for movement meant life. Plotinus had defined beauty as symmetry irradiated by life. The Byzantines agreed with this, and their use of light, and of shade, was intended to make every mosaic, even every bas-relief, shimmer with movement. At the same time the spectator's glance was expected to move. He was not to stare fixedly, but to let his eye wander across and up and down the building or the picture, noting the harmonious sequences of the parts till he could appreciate the whole. A favourite theme of Byzantine philosophy was diversity creating unity.

Saint Sophia was unique. There were no attempts to copy it, in Constantinople or elsewhere. Justinian's other great churches followed other patterns. The church of Saint Irene at

43. Saint Sophia, detail of arcading

44. Saint Irene, Constantinople. Begun 532

Constantinople [44] can be said, more truly than Saint Sophia, to be a domed basilica, perhaps akin to the Lady Juliana Anicia's church of Saint Polyeuct. The restored Church of the Apostles, like the Church of Saint John at Ephesus [45A], was cruciform, formed as it were by two basilicas crossing at right-angles, with a dome over the crossing (which to Procopius seemed also to be suspended from heaven), and lesser domes over the four extremities. Its architect was a certain Eulalius. There were octagonal churches radiating from a central dome, such as Saints Sergius and Bacchus at Constantinople [45B] and San Vitale at Ravenna [46, 47], the latter, and possibly the

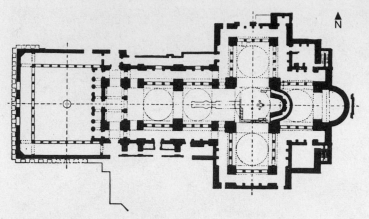

45A. Ground plan of Saint John at Ephesus.
Completed 565. (Plan 1 : 1250)

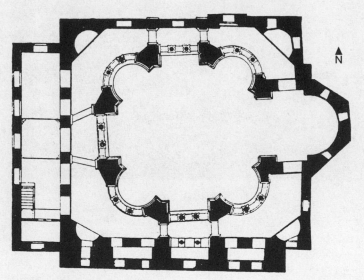

45B. Ground plan of Saints Sergius and Bacchus,
Constantinople. *c.* 525

46 (*opposite*). S. Vitale, Ravenna. 538–45

47 (*above*). S. Vitale, south wall of apse

48. S. Apollinare in Classe, Ravenna. Consecrated in 549

former also, apparently the work of the geometrician Julian Argentarius. There were still straightforward basilicas, such as S. Apollinare in Classe at Ravenna [48]. The decoration of the

49. Detail from frieze,
Saints Sergius and Bacchus, Constantinople. *c.* 525

churches varied. In Constantinople the emphasis seems to have
been at the time more on pattern than on pictorial work.
Nicholas Mesarites, writing of the Church of the Holy Apostles,
says that 'the lines are not plain; they please the senses and
impress the mind by their varied colours and the brilliance of
the gold and the brightness of the lines'. The main decorative
fixture in Saints Sergius and Bacchus was the inscription that
runs round the interior [49]. In the provinces, especially in
Italy, figure-mosaics were usual. This may be due to local
taste, though the great panels of the Emperor and the Empress
in San Vitale were erected to show that their Majesties were
there among their Italian subjects to celebrate the Mysteries.

The minor arts flourished throughout the period, though
'minor' is not an epithet that the Byzantines would have
accepted. As much relative care should be lavished on a carved
ivory or a manuscript illustration as on a church or large
mosaic [50]. It was from the Imperial workshops that the best
products came. It was there that teams of painters illustrated
the purple codices sent out by the Government as gifts to
worthy recipients. It was there that fine ivories were carved and
fine silk woven, especially the ceremonial robes and metal
fruit that were beginning to be the insignia of rank in the
Palace hierarchy, and the ivory diptychs produced yearly as
the symbols of consular authority. Precious materials were

50. The Transfiguration.
Monastery of Saint Catherine on Mount Sinai. *c.* 540

51. Saint Mark. From the Codex Rossanensis. Mid sixth century

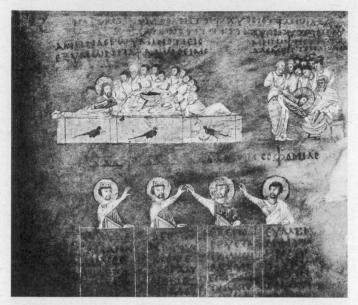

52. The Last Supper and other scenes.
From the Codex Rossanensis. Mid sixth century

53. Rebekah at the well. From the Vienna Genesis. Mid sixth century

54 (*opposite*). The Archangel Michael. Detail from ivory diptych. Early sixth century

55 (*opposite*). A poet. Detail from ivory diptych. Mid sixth century

56. The Communion of the Apostles. Silver paten. 565–78

57. The ivory chair of Archbishop Maximian. *c.* 548

particularly admired, gold for its identification with flame, silver which was regarded as the purest form of white, ivory, coloured stones and marbles, silk with its special sheen. Outside of the Court no one now, at least after Juliana Anicia's death, could afford the cost of the raw materials and the workmanship which was now required. The decoration of the churches of Ravenna was undoubtedly designed and paid for at Constantinople, as was the ivory throne presented to its bishop [57]. No provincial city could have provided such luxuries out of its own revenues. There was certainly popular art. Provincial churches and monasteries saw to their own humble decoration, though they seem often to have used pattern books sent out from the capital. In the capital itself old Greco-Roman traditions continued. A number of sixth-century epigrams exist in praise of popular portraits of charioteers and athletes and actresses.

III

It would be a mistake to draw too strong a distinction between religious and lay art at the time, though little of the latter has survived. A sixth-century Byzantine would have been surprised to hear his religious art described as stiff or hieratic. To him, as to his ancestors, the artist was the *zoographos*, he who draws living things, a man whose craft (*techne*) was required to express the individual nature (*physis*) of the model. Portraits were expected to be portraits. Relative proportions might be disregarded for purposes of respect. But that was already an established tradition, of which we see examples on the column of Theodosius I and on his silver platter, now at Madrid [26, 27, 18]. Not only did the popular epigrammatists praise the verisimilitude of popular drawings, but Procopius, when describing the statue of Theodora set up in Constantinople, emphasizes the excellence of the portrait, though of course it cannot do full justice to the Empress's incomparable beauty. If there is a certain formality in the mosaic panels, this was largely due to technical problems. The mosaicists had not yet learnt to vary the size of their cubes. Unfortunately the mosaics with which Justinian decorated the walls of the Palace hall of the Chalke, depicting the political and military triumphs of his reign, have not survived. The floor-mosaics unearthed in the Palace, which probably date from a little earlier,[1] show the

1. For the date of these mosaics see below, Catalogue of Illustrations, No. 58. To judge from Procopius' description of the Chalke, Justinian preferred marble floors.

Roman-Hellenistic tradition at its most accomplished [58, 59].
It is probable that the paintings in encaustic executed for
Justinian round a palace portico, to depict the famous chariot-
races of his reign, were equally in the old tradition. They were
praised by a state official called Thomas for their wonderful
verisimilitude.

This is all in the Hellenistic tradition. Byzantine civilization
was too firmly embedded in the Greco-Roman past for there

58. Detail from the floor-mosaics in the Great Palace, Constantinople.
Late fifth or early sixth century

to have been an artistic revolution; and secular art could carry
it on without any break. So too could architecture. The
geometrical studies that enabled Anthemius to design Saint
Sophia developed out of studies of the long line of Greek
geometricians to which he was an heir. The theory of optics
that dominated the decorative devices of the age was taken
from Euclid and his school. What was new, what gave the art
of Justinian's time a synthesis that enables us to call it Byzantine
art, is that it was the art of a Christian Empire, centred on and
radiating from a highly intelligent and conscious Court, eager
to express the needs of the Empire and the Church in a manner

59. Detail from the floor-mosaics in the Great Palace, Constantinople. Late fifth or early sixth century

worthy of God and his earthly viceroy. Tastes were certainly changing. Perhaps owing to oriental influences there was a more intense and subtle appreciation of light and of colour than in the past. In spite of the teaching of many of the Christian Fathers, the Neoplatonic theory of beauty was generally accepted, displacing the old Aristotelian view. But these changing tastes triumphed because the Imperial authorities wished and were wealthy enough to carry out a programme of public works of all sorts, from great buildings down to Consular ivories and didactic illustrated manuscripts, and to do so with sumptuous extravagance. Hence it was possible to make

60. Philanthropia.
Detail from the Consular diptych of Clementinus. 513

experiments in architecture or in decoration, but to synthesize them all as expressions of Imperial *philanthropia*. Philanthropy had been expected of Emperors in pagan days, and had even been personified in art-forms [60]. But more was demanded from the philanthropy of the Christian Emperor. It should be shown in gifts from God reaching the whole community through the agency of the Emperor. Justinian himself was deeply aware of his role as Emperor. It is to him above all that the artistic splendour of his reign is due. But behind him, eager to support this essential element in the Imperial Christian government, was the Count of the Sacred Largesse and the whole body of the bureaucracy. The building of Saint Sophia involved an expenditure that was vast even for the Imperial government. But what better example of philanthropy could there be than to erect this glorious temple in the honour of God and for the service of his people?

3
The Triumph of the Image

I

The splendour of Justinian's reign faded soon after the great
Emperor's death. His foreign policy had been as grandiose and
as costly as his building programme, with less enduring results.
His attempted reconquest of the western provinces did little
good for the Empire. Within a generation the Empire could
only keep hold of northern Africa and the Italian lands round
Ravenna, with a shadowy suzerainty over Rome. New
barbarians, the Lombards, had swept across the Alps. Across
the Danube came Avars and Slavs, penetrating into the Greek
peninsula and as far as the walls of Constantinople. The rich
provinces of Syria and Egypt were resentful of rule from
Constantinople and had been alienated by the high taxation
and the religious policy of the Emperors; and in Syria the great
metropolis of Antioch had twice been shattered by earthquake
and once been sacked by the Persians. The Sassanid Kingdom
of Persia, ably led by ambitious Kings, perpetually menaced
the eastern frontier; and the Byzantine armies were hard put to
drive back invasion. Justinian's successors were able men who
did their best. But in 602 a popular riot put on the throne a
savage and incompetent adventurer called Phocas, whose folly
provoked a Persian attack fiercer than any before. For several
years Syria and Egypt were both in Persian hands; the Holy
Cross at Jerusalem had been taken into captivity, and Constantinople itself was under attack from the Avars in Europe
and the Persians in Asia.

The Empire was saved by the efforts of a general of Armenian
origin, Heraclius, who became Emperor in 610 and who by 629
had crushed the Sassanid Kingdom and restored the Holy
Cross to Jerusalem. But the triumph was brief. In 633 the
soldiers of the Prophet Mohammed had begun to pour into

Syria from Arabia. By 638 Syria and Palestine, and by 642 Egypt, were in Arab hands, the Christian population there, now wedded to a separatist Monophysite heresy, making little effort to resist the change of masters. By 670 the Arabs had overrun northern Africa and were advancing into Asia Minor, Constantinople was besieged by land and sea with varying intensity from 673 to 683, and again in 717-18 when it seemed that the Empire was doomed.

Once again a brilliant and tireless Emperor arose to save Constantinople and thus to preserve the Empire – a Syrian, Leo III, incorrectly surnamed the Isaurian. He drove the Arabs back and established a frontier line in eastern Asia Minor, which, though it was often broken by raiders, could be maintained for two centuries till the Arab Empire began to decline.

It is not surprising that these anxious years form the most obscure period in Byzantine art-history. Constantinople had survived intact, and trade suffered less than might have been expected. When the Persian war cut off the old route of the trade from the Far East it found a new route across the steppes of central Asia. The Imperial currency retained its value. But there was little money to spare to be spent on works of architecture or art. It is possible that the surviving figure mosaics in the church of St Demetrius at Thessalonica [61] date from the seventh century and were put up after the city had been saved from a Slav attack by the direct intervention, it was believed, of the saint. But nothing else has survived that can be securely dated to that century.

The absence of material had another cause. Leo III had saved the Empire from the Arabs; but he was to plunge it into a political-religious controversy that was to split it for over a century.

II

In spite of the disapproval expressed by many of the most revered Early Fathers, the taste for pictorial representations of Christ and the Saints increased; and increasing adulation was paid to these images, or icons. The Emperors encouraged icons. It was their policy to use such representations to show the divine source of their power. Coins issued by Justinian II and his successors usually have the Emperor's portrait on the obverse and the head of Christ on the reverse, to emphasize

61. Saint Demetrius and donor.
Saint Demetrius, Thessalonica. Mid seventh century?

62. Gold solidus of Justinian II. Christ on obverse;
the Emperor on reverse. *c*. 690

the intimate connection [62]. The great mosaic of Christ that
Maurice erected over the Chalke, the main entrance to the
Palace, had beneath it portraits of the Emperor and his family
receiving the divine blessing. Icons were credited popularly
with miraculous powers, especially in effecting cures. Lives of
the saints written in the late sixth and seventh centuries are full
of such stories. We hear, for instance, in the Life of Saint
Symeon the Younger of a woman suffering from an issue of

63. Procession of icons. From the Lorsch Gospels. *c*. 800

blood who rightly believed that if she could see the likeness of the saint she would be healed. Icons could perform public services as well. The defeat of the Persians when they besieged Edessa in 544 was soon attributed to the intervention of the miraculous portrait of Christ which he had sent on a handkerchief to King Abgar of Edessa. The Image of Camuliana, a portrait of Christ similarly *acheiropoiete*, not made by human hands, was used as a palladium in several late sixth-century wars and was carried round the walls of Constantinople in solemn procession by the Patriarch at the time of the Avar siege in 626. When the Arabs besieged the city in 717 the image of the Mother of God *Hodegetria*, a work popularly attributed to the brush of Saint Luke the Evangelist, was similarly carried round the walls.

The use of such palladia was probably intended by the authorities to have a psychological rather than a miraculous effect. Orthodox theologians were anxious that the devotion paid to icons should escape the taint of idolatry. By the beginning of the seventh century they had evolved a doctrine that would justify the devotion. This doctrine is largely based on the teaching of the fifth-century mystic whose works were ascribed to Dionysius the Areopagite. According to him the world of the senses mirrors the world of the spirit. 'The essences and orders which are above us are incorporeal . . . Our human hierarchy, on the other hand, is filled with the multiplicity of visible symbols, through which we are led up hierarchically and according to our ability to the unity of God.' This concept is applied a few years later to church-decoration by Bishop Hypatius of Ephesus when he says that some of the faithful are led by material beauty to intellectual beauty and by the light in the sanctuaries to the immaterial light. During the sixth century the doctrine was taken a little further, and use was made of the text in Genesis, I, 27, which says that 'God created man in his own image'. The Early Fathers such as Clement of Alexandria disapproved of the idea that therefore man's bodily form partook of the divine. But at the end of the sixth century we find Leontius of Neapolis in Cyprus, when defending the Church against Jewish accusations of idolatry, saying: 'The image of God is man, and particularly such a man as has received the indwelling of the Holy Ghost. I therefore justly honour and worship the image of God's servants and glorify the house of the Holy Ghost.' In his view the icons of the saints were thus worthy of worship. But neither he nor any of his contemporaries or immediate successors defined the precise nature of the worship to be given to them.

In spite of such pronouncements there were still many Christians, particularly in the eastern provinces of the Empire, to whom religious representational art smacked of idolatry. The old Judaic tradition was still strong. The Monophysite heretics, many of them of Semitic origin, believed that Christ's nature was purely divine. They could not accept that he could be portrayed. The Jews, though many of their synagogues contained pictorial scenes illustrating the scriptures, were opposed to anything that might suggest graven images. The followers of the new faith of Islam were developing an even sterner disapproval of any depiction of the human form made in God's image. The Emperor Leo III, whose traditional surname, 'The Isaurian', is almost certainly due to a copyist's error and should be 'The Syrian', came from the eastern confines of the Empire and had made his early career as commander of eastern regiments. Though he had permitted the parade of the icon of the Virgin in 717, in the crisis of the Arab siege of Constantinople, his sympathies were with his eastern soldiers. There is no need to seek for Jewish or Muslim influences in his decision to abolish the cult of icons. His opponents naturally accused him of being semi-Muslim; it was a good political cry to associate him with the national enemy. But in fact he was following an old tradition that had remained strong in the eastern provinces. It is equally irrelevant to attribute to him, as many historians have done, constitutional or economic motives. He was not acting in order to crush the landed aristocracy and establish a military government dependent on the Emperor. The old aristocracy had already been ruined by the Arab and Slav invasions, and the 'theme system', the military administration of the provinces, had been inaugurated by his predecessors. Nor was it his prime concern to curb the growing wealth of the monasteries. It was only when the monasteries showed bitter opposition to his religious policy that he and his successors took action against them. It was the theological issue that mattered to him and to his subjects, and the artistic issue that was involved in the theological.

It was after his victory over the Muslims that Leo felt secure enough to act on his ideas. In 726 he ordered the destruction of the mosaic figure of Christ over the Palace gate and its replacement by a simple cross. A riot ensued, in which the rioters were mostly women, and an official overseeing the work was killed. Leo took savage revenge; but four years elapsed before he went further. During those years, in spite of the disapproval of the Patriarch, Germanus I, he built up support for his views within the organization of the Church. In 730 he summoned a Council which approved an Imperial decree forbidding all icons of God or the Saints.

Leo based his view on the old Mosaic prohibition of idols. It was wrong to make them and infinitely worse to pay them any form of worship. His opponents retorted that Moses had lived before the Incarnation. Since God had taken on a recognizable human form he could be depicted as could his Mother and his disciples. They protested vigorously; but Leo, secure in the support of the majority of the army and most of the Asiatic provinces, continued to remove religious icons of all sorts in Constantinople and other leading cities, though it is doubtful whether his orders were carried out in Thessalonica or in Greece, and they could not be enforced in Byzantine Italy, where the Roman Papacy would have none of his doctrine. It is unlikely that he had much recourse to actual persecution. Leo died in 741. His son and successor, Constantine V, was a brilliant soldier and administrator but personally unstable in his morals and with strong unorthodox religious views, tinged with extreme Monophysism, with a loathing for Mariolatry, for relics and even for the title of saint, which he forbade to be used. He had no scruples against persecuting his opponents; but he also wished to establish a firm philosophical basis for his Iconoclasm.

This was necessary because his opponents, the so-called Iconodules, had found a spokesman in the greatest theologian of the age, a Christian Arab of Damascus, a former Official in the Caliph's Treasury, called originally Mansur, and after his retirement into a monastery John of Damascus. It was John who formulated the theory which was to govern later Byzantine art. He based his argument on the Neoplatonist doctrine that the appreciation of visible beauty is a necessary though transitory path towards the appreciation of absolute beauty, which is apprehended only by the soul. The visible form is all that the human eye can grasp of the Idea. Thus the Incarnation provides the necessary path along which human souls reach the true knowledge of God. Visible pictures of Christ in his incarnate form help to guide us towards his reality, and are therefore

64A. The Emperor prostrate before Christ.
Saint Sophia, Constantinople. *c.* 890

worthy of reverence, especially as they cannot exist independently of him, any more than a shadow can exist without the form which causes the shadow. But the reverence is paid not to the material object but to the prototype; and the form of reverence should be only *proskynesis* [64], the respectful salutation that is given to holy relics and to consecrated objects and to human beings who symbolize divine authority, such as the Emperor. The Godhead, being infinite, could not be depicted; it is only many centuries later that God the Father is ever shown, and that is incorrect: though there is scriptural justification for depicting the Holy Spirit in the form of a dove. Angels, though ordinarily invisible, can be depicted since they are finite and have been seen by the saints. John also valued the image as 'the book of the illiterate', but this purely didactic aspect was to him of secondary importance. It was, rather, as a channel through which spiritual understanding could pass to the onlooker that the image was important. The images of the saints, too, are to be respected, as are their relics, because the grace of the Holy Spirit which inspired them in their lives lingers round their earthly remains and their portraits. As a reflection of the prototype the image was witness to its presence.

Constantine V met these arguments by summoning a Council in 754 which called itself the Seventh Oecumenical Council – illegally, as neither Rome nor the Eastern Patri-

64B. Detail of 64A

archates were represented. Its pronouncements, dictated to it by the Emperor, were that images could not be legitimate. As Christ had a human and a divine nature combined in a single Person, the image of Christ must either be picturing the divine nature, which is impossible to picture, or it pictures the human nature alone, thus breaking the unity of Christ's person. The Emperor added a curious argument stating that an image if made is of the same substance as the original. But the bread and wine of the Sacrament are the only matter stated by Christ to be of his substance. Lumps of wood or pieces of glass could not be part of Christ's substance, and it was grossly impious to attempt to make them so, This degrading alliance with crude matter applied also to images of the saints, which were therefore equally to be deplored.

The Iconodules had little difficulty in refuting these arguments. The image, they pointed out, was not co-substantial with the original, but was an imitation, or *mimesis* in the Platonic sense, like a shadow, as John of Damascus had pointed out. Also, to deny that Christ in his human nature could be depicted was to deny the Incarnation. It was sheer Monophysism to insist that his single person excluded his visible human nature. It was inevitable that the artists, being mortal, and the materials, being earthly, were unworthy. An epigram written in the tenth century by Constantine of Rhodes on an icon of the Mother of God says: 'If one would paint thee, O Virgin, stars rather than colours would be needed, that thou, the Gate of Light, shouldst be depicted in luminosities. But the stars do not obey the voices of mortals. Therefore we delineate and paint thee with what nature and the laws of painting can provide.' It was the divinity of the original that sanctified this secular imitation. 'Christ is venerated not in the image but with the image,' wrote John of Damascus; or as the author of the life of Saint Stephen wrote: 'The icon is the door opening the God-created mind to the likeness of the original within.'[1]

The Iconodules had the best of the argument. But Iconoclasm, supported by the army, remained the official doctrine

1. There were two phases in the controversy on images, due to the elaboration of Iconoclastic theory under Constantine V. John of Damascus was mainly concerned to show that icons could be revered without involving idolatry. The later Iconodule apologists, such as the Patriarch Nicephorus, were obliged to define the nature of the proper reverence and go more deeply into the philosophical concept of the image.

till 787, when, under the Athenian-born Empress Irene, the Council of Nicaea, the true Seventh Oecumenical Council, reversed it, adopting the doctrine enunciated by John of Damascus. Even so there was sufficient support for Iconoclasm for it to be re-introduced by Leo V in 815. But public opinion

65. Cross in the apse of Saint Irene, Constantinople. *c.* 750

now favoured images, and even the army, where oriental troops were more and more replaced by Slavs, began to lose its Iconoclastic enthusiasm. There was no serious opposition when in 843 the Empress-Regent Theodora restored Orthodoxy at a Council which re-affirmed the findings of the Council of 787.

III

The Iconoclastic Controversy was of fundamental importance in the history of Byzantine art. It resulted in the formulation of an official theory of art which was to remain in force so long as Byzantism lasted, and which was perfectly suited to the Byzantine temperament. It had other effects as well.

The Iconoclastic Emperors were no enemies to art, however much they disliked religious representational art. Unlike the stricter Muslims they did not object to pictures of the human form. On their coins their own portraits were to be seen, but with a simple cross on the reverse. It is probable that they continued to decorate the chambers of the Palace with scenes of their secular triumphs, as Justinian I had done, though they removed portrayals of the Oecumenical Councils. Churches were decorated with pictures of birds and flowers; Constantine V was accused of handing over the Church of the Virgin of Blachernae into the keeping of beasts and birds. In the apse there would usually be a simple cross, such as still survives in the apse of Saint Irene [65].

It is probable that the eighth-century Emperors were not particularly active artistically. But the last Iconoclastic Emperor, Theophilus (829-42), was a builder of the calibre of the

66. Silver coin of Theophilus. c. 830

great Justinian. In particular he added a large number of ceremonial halls to the Imperial Palace, some of them directly inspired by detailed accounts that he had received of buildings in the Abbasid Caliph's capital, Baghdad. These included pavilions to which were given names in the oriental taste, the

'pavilion of the Pearl', the 'chamber of Love', the 'hall of Harmony'. The decoration of these halls was also inspired by the East. There were arabesques and patterns suggested by Cufic inscriptions, but also birds and flowers in mosaic, and scenes that included human figures, which the stricter attitude of Baghdad would not have allowed [67]. In these halls Theophilus placed the mechanical devices with which he and his successors liked to impress visitors from less sophisticated lands, the bronze lions that wagged their tails and roared, the golden birds that sang on silver trees, the throne that rose into the air while the foreign ambassador prostrated himself before the Imperial presence. Here again the inspiration came from the East, though Byzantine technicians added their own improvements.

The church decorations of the Iconoclasts perished. With the triumph of images, patrons hastened to redecorate churches according to the triumphant doctrine. But the secular buildings survived intact, and had their influence on the development of Byzantine taste. In the early Byzantine centuries secular art had continued to follow the Roman-Hellenistic tradition. Illustrated manuscripts of secular authors' works tended to

68 (*opposite*). Bronze doors in the narthex of Saint Sophia, Constantinople. Pre-841

69. Silver bucket. 613-29

reproduce or follow the style of the illustrations of earlier
editions. Surviving secular mosaics, such as those on the floors
of the Great Palace, show a continuity with the past, though the
technique was more accomplished. The Iconoclasts, when they
sought to free themselves from the religious art of the image,
were therefore inclined to fall back on the old Classical style. A
liking for Classical proportion and restraint was re-introduced
and remained after the Iconodule victory; and it was accompanied by a revival of Classical learning. During the
seventh and eighth centuries the standards of Byzantine
scholarship had been low. Leo III was said to have closed the
University, but in any case it had already ceased to be an
intellectual centre. The only towering intellectual figure of the
eighth century had been the theologian John of Damascus, who
lived all his life in the lands of the Muslim Caliphate. The ninth
century saw a remarkable intellectual revival, in philosophy, in
mathematics and in the appreciation of literature. This was

70. Silver dish, with Silenus. 613-29

helped by a not unfriendly rivalry with the intellectual life of the
Baghdad Caliphate, but it was undoubtedly sparked off by the
secularizing policy of the Iconoclastic Court.

It is impossible to regret the collapse of Iconoclasm. Had it
persisted, Byzantine art would have been narrowed, and the
Byzantines would have been denied the right to express in art
their deep religious feelings. Theologically the Iconodules were
justified by the doctrine of the Incarnation, artistically by the
religious art that flourished during the next four centuries. But
the Iconoclastic interlude had its value. By enlarging upon
secular art it recreated a taste for Classical standards. The
exuberance that was beginning to overflow in Justinian's time
was dimmed. The revival of interest in Classical literature and
the secular sciences, especially geometry, gave a desire for
restraint and proportion, which controlled but did not weaken
the intensity of religious inspiration. The grandest epoch in
Byzantine art was to follow.

93

4
The Full Programme

The Classical revival pervaded all the arts. It was not always beneficial. In literature it had the effect of stunting the development of a living literary language. Men of letters sought to reproduce the style and even the vocabulary and syntax of the writers of Classical Greece, but with a flowery profusion derived from orators rather than from writers.[1] The result was an artificiality which few authors were gifted enough to overcome. The level of learning certainly was raised, but, as with literature, admiration for the past tended to inhibit original speculation. In music the revival seems merely to have encouraged the study of musical theory as a branch of philosophy, akin to mathematics, with little reference to musical composition and practice.

In the visual arts the result was happier. Byzantine architects must have always maintained their standards. We know little about the buildings commissioned by the Emperor Theophilus; but they certainly posed constructional problems. The triumph of the Iconodules led to the building of a number of new churches, of which the largest and most famous was the Nea Basilica of the Emperor Basil I. This church did not survive the fall of Constantinople in 1453; but it was fully described soon after its erection by the future Patriarch Photius. It embodied the design known as the Greek Cross. A cross with equal arms is inscribed in a square. The intersection of the arms is crowned with a dome, whose outward thrust is borne by barrel-vaulting or semi-domes over the arms of the cross, and their thrust in turn is borne by the walls that enclose the corners between the arms. These corner chambers might, as in the case of the

---

1. It must be remembered that, before the days of printing, manuscripts were few, and to reach a wide public written works had to be capable of being read aloud; and a bare taut style which an intelligent reader can well appreciate is often too much of a strain on a listener, who needs the time that greater verbosity supplies.

71. The Patriarch Nicephorus victorious over the Iconoclast
John the Grammarian. Detail of miniature. Late ninth century

Nea, each be surmounted by a small light dome whose thrust
was balanced by that of the semi-domes. The result was a
building of admirable geometrical logic. The stresses and
counter-stresses looked after each other. There was no need for
buttressing, and the dome itself could be carried on four
slender piers or even columns, thus leaving the interior un-
cluttered by heavy masonry.

The Greek Cross style was henceforward the most favoured
by Byzantine architects. Usually the apse and the chambers on
either side were affixed on to the square at the east end, balanced
by the narthex at the west end so that the central chamber could
be left open. The square need not be perfect, so long as the
structural integrity was ensured. There was a growing taste for
elegance and a distaste for solid blocks. Straight lines where
they were essential were merged into curves as they soared upwards. The rich decoration of the walls was intended to make

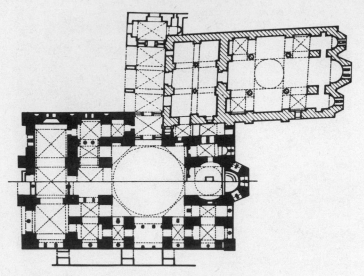

72. Ground plan of the Catholicon and Theotokos,
Hosios Lukas, *c.* 1040

them appear less substantial. The sides of the Church of the
Holy Apostles, according to Mesarites, were 'covered with
many-coloured sawn stone'. 'The stone', he adds, 'was cut to
such thinness that the wall seems to be covered with many-
coloured woven draperies. The stone blooms with such
liquidity that its glistening surface outshines any flower.'
Mesarites similarly compares the white marble of the altar-table
to white linen cloth. The same type of appreciation appears in a
sixth-century epigram on the Church of Saint Polyeuct. 'On
either side of the aisle columns standing on strong columns
support the rays of the golden dome, while arched recesses on
either side dissolving on to the dome reproduce the ever
revolving light of the moon. The walls opposite are clothed in
innumerable paths with wonderful metallic veins of colour, like
flowering meadows that nature has made to flower in the depths
of the rock and has hidden their splendour, keeping them for
the House of God.' But now even the outside of the building,
which earlier architects had left bare, was lightened by blind
arcades and by patterns of brick-work alternating with plaster
and the insertion of glazed tiles and earthenware saucers.

Size for its own sake was not desired. The churches now were
comparatively small, to the surprise of western travellers used

96

to the vastness of their medieval cathedrals. The Nea was a big building, probably about the size of Saint Irene, with surrounding courts and arcades that added to its importance. But it was exceptional. A smaller building was preferred, because it could be comprehended as a whole. Saint Sophia was so huge that many of its details were invisible to a worshipper standing at ground level. He could not see into the gallery with its Imperial portraits; and the mosaic figures of canonized bishops high up on the northern and southern walls below the dome, colossal though they were, would only be clearly visible to the very long-sighted. Saint Sophia, unlike other Byzantine churches, was not only the greatest ceremonial hall of the Sacred Empire but also a gallery housing individual works of art. There alone could mosaic panels such as the Imperial portraits or, above all, the superb Deesis, be seen as single pictures without reference to their surroundings.

Elsewhere the church was planned and, if possible, executed as a whole. The building was conceived as a single vast icon. The victory of the Iconodules and the peace that it brought to the Church led to the stabilization of the Holy Liturgy. It is from the eighth century that the earliest surviving manuscripts of the Liturgy attributed to Saint John Chrysostom, the regular liturgy of the Byzantine Church, and that attributed to Saint Basil, used on certain Fast Dates, are dated. The Liturgy became the central feature of Byzantine religious life. To be deprived of the right to attend the Liturgy was the cruellest punishment that a Byzantine could suffer, and he bitterly resented any attempt to alter or to supersede it. The later Byzantine hostility to the Roman Church was due, more than anything else, to the Roman hierarchs' desire to impose their liturgy on the Easterners. The Liturgy was the daily representation of Christ's Passion on earth; and the church building was the scene of this representation. It was therefore holy with a triple symbolism. It was holy as a consecrated building in which the Divine Mysteries could be celebrated. It was holy because it embodied the whole Liturgical year. Christ's life on earth was represented in images of the great Feasts of the Church, the Twelve Mysteries,[1] betokening the main events of his life and the life of his Mother, of which the scenes were usually placed in the narthex, the ante-church, as an introduction to the main holy story. The worshipper could thus trace the whole story of the

1. Sometimes fifteen, with additional scenes from the life of the Mother of God.

74. Archangel Gabriel, Daphni. *c.* 1020

Incarnation in its proper sequence as he gazed around him. Finally the church, as the setting of the Incarnation and the Passion, itself represented the universe into which Christ descended. The dome was heaven, from which Christ Pantocrator, the Ruler of All, looked down, sometimes benignly, sometimes, as in the church at Daphni, with the sternness of an all-seeing judge [73]; and on the high ceilings round the dome the angels floated [74]. In his description of the Church of the Holy Apostles, Mesarites, writing in the late twelfth century, says that the central space, redecorated after the end of Iconoclasm, 'can really be called the dome of Heaven, since the Sun of Justice shines in it, the light which is above light, the Lord of Light, Christ Himself'. The twelve apostles, or it might be the Patriarchs of the Old Dispensation, supported the dome. The apse was the cave of Bethlehem, and in it was the Mother of God with her Child. The altar was the table of the Last Supper, the ciborium above it the holy sepulchre. Round the walls were the images of the saints, each in his suitable place, betokening the Church on earth. All these images, as visible shadows of invisible Beings, showed that Christ and his saints were present at the Eucharist.

75. The Mother of God, Saint Sophia, Constantinople.
Late ninth century

The arrangement was not uniform except for the Pantocrator
in the dome and the Mother of God in the apse [75]. The major
saints were always shown, but not always in the same place;
minor saints were varied, according to local interests and to the
devotional tastes of the founder of the building. But the general
scheme and its meaning were everywhere accepted. The church
building and all its decoration were integrated with the Liturgy.
No part was to be considered in isolation.

The theory had its practical results. There was less than ever
a place for free statuary in Byzantine churches. It was never
banned. A few holy statuettes were still carved, probably to be
placed in some niche in a private oratory, where they would
only be seen frontally [76]. Bas-relief was frequently used to

76. The Mother of God 'Hodegetria'. Twelfth century

decorate a screen or a balustrade; and even holy images might be carved in bas-relief, to fill some spot where the slight shadows of the carving would be especially effective. But the proper effect of the decoration of the church was gained by pictorial as opposed to sculptural work.

The image was there to show that the prototype was present at the Liturgy and to provide a channel through which the worshipper could reach the prototype. It therefore must face the ceremony and the worshipper. The body itself did not have to be shown frontally, but if the body was drawn turning away,

77. Moses receiving the Law. Miniature from a Psalter. Mid tenth century

the head must be drawn so that the eyes can see and be seen. Even in the pictorial scenes from the life of Christ, where it is the whole picture rather than any one character in it which is the image, only the ungodly such as Judas have their faces drawn in profile. The holy figures, even if the composition demands that the bodies are in profile – as for instance that of the Mother of God lying on her bed at the Koimesis, the Assumption – have their faces turned slightly towards the on-looker. The convention was not, however, fully extended to illuminated manuscripts, where the drawings were perhaps not regarded as images in the full sense. There the Evangelists are sometimes shown in profile at their desks. Moses is in profile when he receives the tablets of the Law on Sinai and other Old Testament figures are also sometimes in profile [77, 78]. It is

78. Saint Matthew at his desk. Miniature from a Gospel. Twelfth century

LINACRE COLLEGE LIBRARY
UNIVERSITY OF OXFORD

likely that immediately after the Iconodule victory the fashion was to decorate the churches only with single figures. The descriptions of the Nea suggest that there were no biblical scenes in it; and there are none in Saint Sophia. The desire to depict Feasts of the Liturgical year seems to have arisen during the tenth century.

The medium had to match the subject. Just as sight was the first of the senses, so light was the first of the elements. Sight needed light, and light to the Byzantines meant colour, and colour distinguished form. This gave the supremacy to pictorial art. But while painting in fresco continued throughout the period, it was overshadowed by mosaic work. The Byzantines' eager study of optics meant above all the study of light. The glass mosaic could catch and reflect the light as no other medium could. Beams of light coming from well sited windows and spaces in the architecture would enhance its effect; and especially in the glimmer of lamps and candles the whole picture seemed to move. During the grey days of the bleak Constantinopolitan winter it must have been an impressive experience to come in from the dark windswept street and see the saints glowing with life in the light of the flickering flames. The technique of the mosaicist had steadily improved. Now he used glass tesserae of varying sizes, set at varying angles, inserting occasional cubes of marble or some semi-precious stone to alter the effect. Each composition was carefully calculated to look at its best to a worshipper of average height standing in about the centre of the church. His eye was expected to pass round the sequence of saints and scenes, each individual picture being merged into the general effect.

It is not always easy to achieve delicate drawing and modelling in mosaic; and the insistence on frontal portraiture might have been expected to produce a stiffness of effect. The skill of the mosaicists of the tenth and eleventh centuries enabled them to overcome these difficulties. The Classical revival introduced by the Iconoclasts survived and was enhanced. The proportions were increasingly elegant and graceful. If we compare the solid, rather squat Mother of God in the apse of the church of Saint Sophia at Thessalonica, erected possibly soon after the Council of Nicaea in 787, but more probably immediately after the final victory of images half a century later, with the Mother of God in the apse of Saint Sophia at Constantinople, erected a few years later by Imperial craftsmen, we can watch how taste is

79. Donor with the Mother of God. Frontispiece to a Gospel. *c.* 1100

81. South vestibule opening into the narthex of Saint Sophia, Constantinople, with mosaic of the Mother of God. Probably *c.* 1000

moving [81]. The Mother of God in the apse, delicate though she is, looks a little inadequate to fill the great curve in which she sits. If we compare her in her turn with the Mother of God between the two Emperors in the porch, erected at the end of the tenth century, we see the triumph of the Classical ideal.

II

This taste could be expressed because all the major works of art were produced under the aegis of the Imperial Court. Many of the Emperors were highly educated men with cultured tastes, such as Leo VI, the Wise, and Constantine VII, Porphyrogenitus. Even usurping Emperors of humble origin, such as Basil I, who never learnt to write properly, knew the value of art, if only as propaganda, as Basil's building of the Nea testifies. The great soldier-Emperor Basil II was, it is true, a philistine who resented spending money on the arts. But even if the Emperor were uninterested, the production of works of art was guaranteed by the civil service, a body of highly intelligent men chosen for their intellectual achievements, trained to regard art as a proper expression of religious truth and of Imperial prestige. The art of the time was sumptuous and expensive. Stone and brick and mortar might be comparatively cheap, but the marble needed for columns and for the lining of the interior of the building was not cheap. The decoration of even quite a small church involved several million mosaic cubes. A large glass factory was required to supply them. Silk hangings worthy of a sanctuary would have to be produced by the silk-works of the Palace. Private looms were not able, and were not allowed, to weave brocade of the first quality. Carpets might come from private factories, such as that owned at Patras in the Peloponnese by the widow Danelis, who presented a carpet woven at her works to the Emperor for use in Saint Sophia.

Even the smaller works of art, the carved ivory panels, the enamel plaques and reliquaries, the metal bowls and chalices,

82. Gold and enamel armband. Ninth century

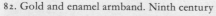

83. Gold filigree earrings. Probably ninth century

84. Onyx paten with an enamel medallion
depicting the Last Supper. *c.* 900

85 (*above*). Reliquary for fragments of the True Cross. Mid tenth century

86. Silk shroud of Saint Germain. Tenth century

87. Onyx chalice. *c.* 1000

were produced by the Palace factories. Private manufacturers could not afford the raw material. Manuscripts were still copied and illustrated in the monasteries, but the finest illuminated manuscripts came from the Palace workshops, as did the finest textiles, intended as hangings for the churches or ceremonial robes for the Court. The same artistic conventions as in the Church decoration were preserved. Christ blessing the Emperor on an ivory panel looks out full face at the viewer, though here the Emperor will modestly bow his head [88]. The saints depicted on an enamelled reliquary are the miniature copies of the saints on a mosaic wall.

It was inevitable therefore that art should reflect the tastes of the cultured circles that ran the government. How Classical these tastes were can be seen by such religious manuscripts as the Psalter now in Paris probably to be dated about 970, where not only the personified elements such as Night and Dawn but biblical figures such as David are shown in completely Classical guise [89]. It is, naturally, still more striking in the secular works

88. Constantine VII crowned by Christ. 945

ΓΑΘΑ
ΝΑΗΛ   ΡΑΔ   ΧΑΔ

ΕΛΙΑΒ   ΙΕCCΑΙ   ΔΑΔ

89. King David. Miniature from a psalter. Mid tenth century

that have survived. We know very little of the decoration of the
Imperial Palace, apart from the mechanical devices that so
greatly impressed such foreign visitors as Liutprand of
Cremona. It was the Sacred Palace, and many of its halls were

90. Saint Demetrius. Enamel medallion.
Mid eleventh century

used for ceremonies that were almost as religious as any in the
churches. In such halls God and the Saints would be present in
their images, as well as the holy Emperors of the past. In the
halls intended for secular use there were probably mosaics
representing the triumphs of the Emperor and his ancestors. In
the twelfth century the Emperor Manuel I had such scenes set
up in his palace at Blachernae.

The popular epic of the Digenis Akritas describes the decoration of an ideal noble residence. It is a building of vaulted

91 (*top*). Detail of the Veroli Casket. Tenth or eleventh century

92. Enamelled glass bowl, with mythological figures. Eleventh century

chambers and marble columns, the rooms gleaming with golden mosaics, and mosaic scenes showing stories from the Old Testament, Moses and Joshua and David and Goliath, from Homer, Agamemnon and Achilles, Odysseus and the Cyclops, Penelope and her suitors, as well as stories of the life of Alexander the Great. The poet undoubtedly had in mind the chambers in the Emperor's palace. The style of such works stemmed from the late Iconoclastic style, Classical and as realistic as the medium allowed. Smaller secular works such as ivory caskets intended for lay use seem often wholly Classical in their inspiration. The tenth-century Veroli Casket with its *putti* might have been made in Hellenistic times [91]. The dark red glass bowl in the Treasury of Saint Mark's in Venice, probably of about the same date, is perhaps even more typical of the taste of the time [92]. Its polychrome enamelling is Byzantine, the decoration round the rim is derived from the Cufic alphabet of the Muslims, but the figures on it seem to have been copied from an ancient Greek vase.

No provincial house can have been as splendid as the fictional palace of Digenis Akritas. The border barons lived in grim castles, with perhaps a few frescoes and tapestry hangings as decoration. The great nobility, though they owned large estates by the end of the tenth century, never lived on them from choice. They hated to be away from the centre of power and intrigue at the capital, and seem to have taken little trouble over their country seats. There were certainly rich provincial magnates who enjoyed a comfortable luxury, but they had neither the raw materials nor the technicians at hand to fill their houses with carved marbles or mosaics. Provincial churches, except for a few Imperial foundations for which the craftsmen and materials were sent out from Constantinople, were decorated with frescoes, according to the principles that were now accepted. The artists seem usually to have been local monks, though there may have been itinerant painters travelling from place to place and transmitting the fashions of the time, while drawings or illuminated manuscripts could provide models for figures and decorative schemes. But on the whole the provincial monastic artist was suspicious of the modish intellectuals of Constantinople, and uninterested in Classical refinement. The images that he painted, after due prayer, were there to play their part in the liturgy. It did not matter if their drawing was clumsy and their colouring simple. The sincerity

93. Cave church near Göreme, Cappadocia.
Ninth–tenth centuries

of the feeling that inspired them, as in some of the Cappadocian
cave-churches, transcends any crudity in technique. The artists
knew what effect they wished to achieve, and they achieved it.

III

No people have ever more deeply revered and respected art than
the Byzantine people at the height of their medieval prosperity.
It is therefore remarkable that no great respect was paid to the
artist. He remained anonymous. The only architect of the
period whose name has survived is the Armedian Tirdat, who
was called in to repair the cracked dome of Saint Sophia at the
end of the tenth century. Of the artists who designed and
executed the great mosaic panels we know nothing. The

118

Menologion of the Emperor Basil II, copied in about A.D. 1000, contains the signatures of eight of the artists who painted the miniatures; and the name of the illuminator, Theodore of Caesarea, is given in a manuscript dated 1066. It is possible that such miniaturists also supplied the designs for mosaics and therefore enjoyed a little prestige; but to the Byzantine of the time the artist's person was of no importance. The greatest works of art were produced by the workmen of the Palace schools. The artist was simply a civil servant engaged, as were all the civil servants, in enhancing the glory of God and his Sacred Empire on earth; but of too junior rank to appear in any list of Imperial officials. He was not regarded as a creator. He was simply the channel through which art flowed. To the Iconodule theorist, Patriarch Nicephorus of Constantinople, a picture had five causes, the 'poetic', the 'organic', the 'formal', the 'material' and the 'final'. The 'poetic' cause probably meant the patron who commissioned the work of art, that is to say, in most cases, the Emperor. The 'organic' cause meant the artist who carried it out. The 'formal' cause is the most important. It is the subject of the picture, which is itself only the shadow or image of the prototype. The 'material' cause must be literally the material of which the picture is made, the mosaic cube or the paints. The 'final' cause is the most difficult to interpret. Probably Nicephorus intended it to be the purpose or function of the picture.[1]

Such a theory did not rate the artist very high. He was just carrying out his patron's wishes, and he was restricted by growing conventions in iconography. Colour was increasingly used to identify characters and scenes. The Mother of God was clothed in blue or purple shades, Saint Paul in light green and blue. Christ must be clad in white for the Transfiguration and blue and gold for scenes before the Crucifixion and purple and gold after the Resurrection. In biblical scenes each figure began to have its proper place and its proper gesture. Yet despite the rules for composition and colouring there was room for that individual treatment which distinguishes a great artist from a lesser one. We can only hope that the former was properly appreciated and rewarded by his patron.

1. I owe this interpretation to Father Gervase Mathew who suggests that this theory derives from a handbook version of Aristotle's *Metaphysics*, Book II, where a fourfold causality is analysed.

The actual technique of making a mosaic panel is not certain. Probably the master-artist drew the original design, and either he or a master-craftsman copied it out in scale on to the plaster, and the craftsmen then hastened under his supervision to insert the cubes before the plaster dried. The ordinary craftsmen, as we know from the early tenth-century *Book of the Prefect*, ranked as *ergolaboi*, men who worked by contract, the employers supplying the material and paying part of the wages in advance, and who were liable to punishment if they broke their contracts. Joiners, plasterers, stonemasons, locksmiths and painters are lumped together. But *ergolaboi* may not have been used in works carried out by the Emperor. The Palace mosaicists were probably not independent workmen but the servants of the Emperor, as were the workers in the Palace silk-factory, whose position was little better than that of slaves, though as employees in the Sacred Palace they must have enjoyed a certain prestige.

Religion and art reached their most complete integration in this period between the ninth and later eleventh centuries. There was a danger that the integration might lead to sterility. Religion, after all, deals with eternal and unchanging truths. Ought art therefore to change? Fortunately the Byzantine artists continued to make experiments, both in technical devices and in composition. The taste for biblical scenes, with their didactic message, increased; and though the scenes had to contain stereotyped figures and general arrangement, there was room to alter the balance of the composition and the colours. There were experiments in perspective, a problem for which the Byzantines evolved many solutions, trying sometimes a box perspective, in which figures were, as it were, formed in isolation, sometimes a perspective of separate planes, sometimes an inverted perspective as though the spectator was looking at the picture from behind. The devices seem strange to eyes trained to accept the perspective adopted in the West at the time of the Renaissance; but each had its mathematical logic.

The desire for experiment was, however, restricted by the intense conviction that the Empire represented an eternal pattern. The art of this great Imperial period must be seen in association with the life at the Imperial Court, a life of fixed ceremonies and slow-moving processions through which, in the words of the Emperor Constantine Porphyrogenitus, the 'Imperial power could be exercised in harmony and order', and 'the Empire could thus reflect the motion of the Universe as it

was made by the Creator'. Constantine's great work on the
Ceremonies gives in detail the proper rites for every feast-day
of the Church and for every Imperial investiture. We are told
exactly who should form each of the processions, and in what
order, where the cortège should pause for the Emperor to
receive ritual gifts and acclamations, and who should give
them, and what the object or the words should be. We are told
of the gestures that the Emperor should make as he moves into
the Palace or one of the great churches, where he should turn
and when he should bow, and on whom he should bestow the
kiss of peace.

The whole ceremonial life of the Court was passed in a sort of
ballet. One of Constantine's most remarkable chapters describes the actual dances, ritual movements rather than dances
in the modern idiom, which were performed at the banquet held

94. Miniature from an early eleventh-century *Cynegetica* of Oppian

95A and B. Enamel plaques from a crown
sent by the Emperor Constantine IX to Hungary. *c.* 1050

on the Emperor's or the Empress's name-day. 'The dinner', he says,

takes place in the most glorious triclinium of Justinian, with the Imperial table separate. The sovereigns take their place at the table, and the usual ritual of the dinner is followed. After the roasts have been served the artoclines go out and introduce those who should perform in the dance, namely the Domestic of the Schools and that of the Numeri, the Demarch of the Blues and his party, the tribunes and the vicars. When these have entered within the doorway they acclaim the sovereigns, wishing them many years; and the Domestic of the Schools presents in his right hand the book of permission. The prefect of the table steps down and takes it, and gives it to the chamberlain in charge of the water. The members of the party say an *apelatikon*, in the first mode . . . The prefect of the table then turns and stretches out his right hand, opens his fingers in the form of rays and closes them again to form a bunch; and the Domestic of the Schools begins to dance with the Domestic of the Numeri, the Demarch, the tribunes, the vicars and the demotes, turning three times round the table. You must know that the tribunes and vicars wear a blue and white garment, with short sleeves, and gold bands, and rings on their ankles. In their hands they hold what are called *phengia*.

After having danced three times, all go down and stand at the foot of the sovereigns' table. Then the singers sing: 'Lord, strengthen the Empire for ever' and the people sing three times 'Lord, strengthen the Empire for ever' . . . The second dance: the party of the Greens enter, following the ceremonial given above, with the Domestic of the Excubites, the Count of the Walls, the tribunes, the vicars and the demotes of the party. You must know that this dance is accomplished according to the ritual given above, without any change, except that the tribunes and vicars wear a garment of green and red, split, with short sleeves and gold bands.[1]

---

1. The 'dance' must have been a stylized walk. The anklets must have been intended to clang as the figures moved. What the *phengia* were is uncertain; they were probably not cymbals, as has been suggested, but some sort of ceremonial torch. The Domestics of the Schools and the Numeri were high military officials attached to the Court, the Domestic of the Excubites and the Count of the Walls high military officials attached to the city. The parties of the Blues and the Greens with their demarchs, tribunes and vicars, and the demotes, who were the ordinary members, were the circus factions of earlier centuries which had now become regiments of local municipal militia. As the colour of their garments shows, the Blues had amalgamated with the still older faction of the Whites and the Greens with the faction of the Reds.

Had the Empire remained at the peak of prosperity and prestige that it enjoyed in the early eleventh century, the ceremonies and all the artistic expression of its faith might have stood still. But Byzantium was to undergo experiences in the later eleventh century that shook its stability and its complacency. In the turmoil taste began to change. With their confidence in the sacred order of their destiny sapped, the Byzantines began to indulge in fantasy on the one hand and on the other a greater humanism.

5
The Changing World

I

The great days of Imperial Byzantium came to an end in the later eleventh century. The centralized and hieratic system of government which had been effective in preserving the Empire in times of trouble proved inadequate when the Empire passed from the defensive to the offensive. The provinces were secure now from raids from across the frontiers; and land became a good investment. A landed aristocracy emerged, of families founded by some successful soldier or statesman whom the State had rewarded with estates, or by some wealthy financier or merchant; and, in spite of legislation intended to curb the process, these families began to increase their holdings by taking over free peasant communities which found the burden of taxation imposed by Constantinople too hard to bear. The central bureaucracy had in the past controlled the provinces by controlling the purse-strings. Now the provincial aristocracy was rich enough not only to defy the bureaucracy but also to buy the services of the local militia, whose pay from Constantinople had been niggardly and slow. This development of a sort of feudal structure came at a moment when the great Macedonian dynasty was petering out under two elderly heiresses, the voluptuous and much-married Zoe and the austere spinster Theodora; and the throne lay open to adventurers. Then, while the government was disorganized by faction and intrigue and the struggle of the landed nobility against the bureaucracy, the Empire had to face simultaneously Norman attacks on its Italian possessions and, worse, the invasion of Turkish hordes, led by the Seljuk dynasty, into Asia Minor. The Normans, who were not much more than an enterprising band of military adventurers, conquered Southern Italy but were eventually driven back when they tried to invade the Balkan peninsula. But, owing to political and military mismanagement, resistance in the East was ineffectual; and soon the whole of Asia Minor was overrun by Turkish settlers. By the end of the century the coast-lands were recovered, but the centre of the peninsula was firmly in Turkish occupation. Byzantium no longer controlled the lands that had been its main source of man-power and food.

The Empire was saved by an Emperor of genius, Alexius I Comnenus (1081–1118). By remarkable diplomatic skill and by a judicious but economical use of military force he defeated the Normans and drove back the Turks and dealt successfully with barbarian invasions from across the Danube. He had hoped to obtain the help of mercenaries from the West but instead was faced with the First Crusade, led by princes, some of them Normans, who were interested not in helping him against the Turks but in carving out principalities for themselves further to the East. The Crusading movement was to bring Byzantium more trouble than aid; but in the meantime Alexius made full use of it. By the end of his reign Constantinople seemed as rich and lively as it ever had been.

But it was the capital of a changed Empire now. The struggle had been hard, and it had left scars. Money had been at times so short that Alexius had been obliged to issue a debased coinage and to confiscate church treasures in order to melt them into bullion. The Palace workshops were brought to a standstill and never reopened on the old scale. The Emperor himself had become a less hieratic figure. From economy and from pressure of other tasks he could no longer keep up the ceaseless stream of ceremonies so lovingly described by Constantine Porphyrogenitus. Their number had declined under the warrior Emperors of the late tenth century, who were too often away campaigning to maintain them: though Basil II's brother, the co-Emperor Constantine VIII, had loved to preside over them in Basil's absence. Under Alexius very few survived. In the full and intimate biography that his daughter, Anna Comnena, wrote of him, there is barely a mention of a ceremonial procession or liturgy. The Emperor's life had become more informal. The Comneni were merely the most successful but not the most distinguished of the noble families of the time. The Ducae, for example, who had a far more celebrated history, were not going to pay Alexius the awe-struck respect that earlier Emperors had commanded. Even Anna Comnena, devoted as she was to the idea of the Empire, was more deeply impressed by nobility of birth and the high standard of manners and education that nobility involved. She regarded her father as the Viceroy of God less because of his Imperial role than because of his superiority of character. Even the old Imperial Palace began to

96. The Empress Irene Ducaena. *c.* 1100

be abandoned. No longer tied to it by the ceremonies that had been held in its courts and the processions that moved from it to Saint Sophia across the square, the Emperors preferred to live at the smaller and more compact Palace of Blachernae, some three miles from Saint Sophia, up against the land-walls by the Golden Horn.

It is not known to what extent the Palace workshops survived. There is no further mention of them. The Imperial Court continued to be the main patron of art, especially under Alexius' splendour-loving grandson, Manuel I, whose lavish mosaic-decoration of the Blachernae Palace proves that there were still great glass-factories in the capital. But patronage was no longer so monolithic.[1] Other magnates besides the Emperor and Empress commissioned the building or the decoration of churches and monasteries or had manuscripts illuminated for them. Rich provincial governors brought artists from Constantinople to adorn their foundations. In the capital, high-placed civil servants were soon to outdo the Emperors in the magnificence of their patronage. To such men the identification of the Imperial Court with the Courts of Heaven was irrelevant.

The change in attitude went deeper. It was as if the Empire had lost some of its self-confidence in its role as the serene microcosm of Heaven on earth. There was a growing awareness of human frailty and the cruelty of fate. The disasters that beset Byzantium could only be explained as divine punishment for the wickedness of mankind, against which the heroism of the saintly was of little avail. A note of pathos creeps in. To Anna Comnena there was something heroically pathetic in the thwarted attempts of her father to combat the evil that was everywhere around him, while for herself she indulged in shameless self-pity, as an old woman exiled from the Court, drowsing as she toiled over her book by lamplight. It is very different from the confident cynicism of Michael Psellus, two generations earlier.

The humanism and the pathos were reflected in the art of the period. Byzantine art of the twelfth century is difficult to judge, as there are practically no survivals of Constantinopolitan work

1. There had always been a few private foundations, such as the church, monastery and hostel founded by the tenth-century admiral Constantine Lips. But this was a very modest affair until it was refounded by the Empress Theodora, wife of Michael VIII.

of the period. Many of the splendid Sicilian and Venetian mosaics are certainly the product of Greek artists. But no self-respecting Greek would leave Constantinople if he could help it. An artist who was ready to settle in Palermo or in Venice must have despaired of making a success of his career in the Imperial City. It might be possible for an Imperial governor to persuade an artist to come and decorate a particular church in his province, as did the Prince Alexius Comnenus for the little church of Nerez in Northern Macedonia or one or two Dukes of Cyprus for their favourite chapels in the island. We still have a few illuminated manuscripts and a few individual works of art that clearly come from the workshops of Constantinople; and that is all.

Yet it is enough to show a steady change in style. The change is foreshadowed in the mosaics of the monastery church of Daphni, near Athens, which from their high quality are clearly the work of artists from Constantinople, and which can probably be ascribed to a date in the 1070s, in the lull before the years of desperate crisis.[1] Here, the great Christ Pantocrator in the dome has a stern, almost terrifying, unworldliness in the old tradition, but the figures in the larger panels have an elegance and a liveliness that is new. There were two other churches in Greece that had already been decorated by mosaicists from Constantinople. But at Holy Luke in Styris, though the technique of the work is high, the drawing and the colouring seem almost like the work of an artist of the Cappadocian school [97]. Therein they no doubt reflected the austere tastes of the Emperor Basil II who commissioned them. At the Nea Moni on Chios, built at the order of the Emperor Constantine IX in

1. For the date of the Daphni mosaics see below, Catalogue of Illustrations, No. 99. But it is most improbable that an Emperor as prudent and as hard pressed for money as Alexius I would have ordered and exported costly mosaics to a province as precariously held as was Greece at the time of the Norman invasions, from 1081 until well into the twelfth century, over seas that were, at least from 1085 to 1095, overrun by Turkish pirates based on Smyrna. Both on historical and stylistic grounds, comparing the mosaics with the Chrysostom manuscript whose date we know, I would date the decoration of Daphni at about 1075, under the Emperor Michael VII, who was temperamentally far more likely than Alexius to have indulged in such patronage and who did not yet realize the problems that the Empire had to face. There is also literary evidence for dating them before 1080. There is unfortunately no evidence connecting any of the Emperors or Empresses or even any high Court official with Daphni or Athens.

97 (*opposite*). Holy Luke the Styriote. *c.* 1020

98. The Anastasis. Nea Moni on Chios. Mid eleventh century

about 1045, the technique is even finer, but it is used with a violence, an angularity of drawing and fiercely contrasted colours unparalleled in Byzantine art [98]. Here there is still a static quality in the composition. Movement was to be obtained by the play of light on the mosaics and in the processional sequence of the figures. At Daphni there is for the first time an attempt to suggest movement by the composition within each panel, while faces and attitudes reflect, very delicately, a touch of human emotion [99]. A similar stirring of humanism is to be seen, in a different medium, in the illuminations of the Homilies of John Chrysostom, executed for the Emperor Nicephorus Botaniates in 1078 [100].

In the south gallery of Saint Sophia there is a mosaic panel, erected in about 1030, of Christ standing between the Empress Zoe and her first husband, Romanus III, whose head was subsequently altered to represent her third husband, Constan-

99. The Birth of the Mother of God. Daphni. *c.* 1075

100. The Emperor Nicephorus Botaniates and the Empress Maria the Alanian. *c.* 1078

101. Christ enthroned between the Emperor Constantine IX
and the Empress Zoe. South gallery of Saint Sophia. *c.* 1028–42

tine IX [101]. It is a weak, conventional work, which suggests
that the old Imperial style was becoming sterile. Nearby is a
similar panel, dating from 1118, showing the Virgin between
the Emperor John II Comnenus and his Empress Irene [102].
The difference in style is striking. The figures are no longer
expressionless. The Virgin combines her divinity with an air of
supreme compassion, while the Imperial couple are portrayed
as human beings, for all their magnificence. The portrait of
their son, added a few years later, is almost poignant in its
depiction of a delicate youth who was to die before he could
succeed to the throne.

No other twelfth-century mosaic has survived in Constantinople. Many were set up. We know that the Church of the
Pantocrator, the favourite foundation of the Comneni, was
splendidly decorated; and Benjamin of Tudela greatly admired
the secular panels, depicting battle scenes, with which Manuel I
adorned the Palace of Blachernae. For the finest twelfth-
century mosaic work we must go to Torcello, in the lagoons

134

102A (*top*). The Mother of God between the Emperor John II Comnenus and the Empress Irene the Hungarian. South gallery of Saint Sophia. *c.* 1118

102B. Detail of 102A

103A. The Mother of God. Torcello. Mid twelfth century

near Venice. The two great mosaics in the Cathedral there are
undoubtedly the work of a first-class Greek artist, who was,
maybe, specially hired by the Venetian government, for none
of his work appears elsewhere in Venice; and they undoubtedly
represent the Byzantine taste of the time. The tall, slender
Virgin in the apse is elongated beyond the optical requirements
of the curve in which she stands; and her divinity is enhanced
by the golden emptiness around her [103]. But her face is
humanly compassionate, the face of a young mother. At the
other end, in contrast, is a Last Judgement [104]. The composition is crowded but carefully balanced and highly dramatic.
Though the drawing shows a touch of fantasy, the pose and
expression of each figure are individually planned. The theme
was fairly new to Byzantine art; but it was carried out with
assurance. In earlier depictions of the Last Judgement the
symbolism of the sheep and the goats had been used. Now
taste demanded a more realistic humanity.

104A. The Last Judgement. Torcello. Mid twelfth century

104B (*opposite*). Detail of 104A

105. Mantle of King Roger II of Sicily. 1133-4

It is harder to evaluate the twelfth-century mosaics in Sicily. There was certainly a group of highly accomplished Greek craftsmen working there in the 1140s, who almost certainly came from Constantinople and probably brought their designs with them. But, except in the church of La Martorana [106], built by a Greek-born admiral and intended for the Greek rite, and designed architecturally as a centralized building of the 'Greek cross' type, these artists were decorating churches of a different order. The earliest mosaics in the cathedral at Cefalù and in the Cappella Palatina at Palermo are roughly of the same date as those in the Martorana. But both these churches are basilicas. In longitudinal basilicas, such as were still being erected in the Byzantine provinces, if there were no dome, the apse was the place of honour; and the Pantocrator was placed there, usually with the Mother of God on a lower panel beneath him. This practice was followed at Cefalù [107]; but in the Cappella Palatina, which was a domed basilica, the Pantocrator appears both in the dome and in the apse, and beneath him in the apse, where now there is an eighteenth-century Mother of God, there was a window. The mosaicists had therefore to adapt their scheme [108]. As a result, only the Martorana gives the impression of being a Byzantine shrine. Its mosaics have a gentle intimacy and grace. They seem, for all their charm, a little weak if we compare them with those of Daphni; but we

106 (*opposite*). Koimisis (Death of the Mother of God). Martorana, Palermo. *c.* 1148

107 (*above*). Pantocrator. Cefalù Cathedral. 1148

108. Cappella Palatina, Palermo. 1143-54

109. The Creation of the Birds and Fishes. Monreale Cathedral. *c.* 1185

have nothing of their date at Constantinople with which to compare them. The mosaics in the apse at Cefalù are on a grander scale; but even the great Pantocrator, though beautifully executed, is melancholy rather than majestic, without the strength of the Pantocrator at Daphni. The Cappella Palatina seems to have undergone three separate stages in its decoration, the later work being carried out by local craftsmen, and there have been modifications in the original design. Moreover, much of the work has been marred by later restoration. The whole effect is of glittering splendour; but the individual panels lack the vigour of the best Byzantine work.

The greatest of the Sicilian churches, the cathedral at Monreale, dates from about 1185. The craftsmen who decorated the huge basilica were almost certainly Greek, though native workmen may have been used for some of the less important panels. But the work seems curiously uncharacteristic of Byzantium. In the first place, the long walls are covered with mosaics, as though hung with tapestries, without the architectural setting or the marble frames or even the fields of gold or plain colour that Byzantine taste demanded [109]. The optical angle has been considered; the upper panels are more broadly drawn and more brightly coloured than the lower; but the decoration bears no functional relationship to the architecture. In the second place the colours are uncharacteristic of what we know of Byzantium. The gold is curiously dark; grey and brown tones predominate; and even the brighter tints are somewhat muted. It is possible that both the design and the colouring reflect the tastes of the Norman king, William II. It is also possible that the craftsmen and the mosaic tesserae were imported to Sicily after the Norman sack of Thessalonica in 1185. Though the building was more or less complete by 1183, the decoration seems barely to have been finished when William died in 1189; and the Normans were never averse to carrying off useful technicians and raw material. It may therefore be that the colouring reflects Thessalonian taste of the close of the twelfth century. The panels themselves are vigorous and lively but a little cruder than the earlier work in Sicily.

The Greek craftsmen who found themselves working in the eclectic civilization of Norman Sicily cannot be regarded as necessarily reflecting the best Byzantine art of the time. But the style of the Monreale mosaics is paralleled by the frescoes, painted by Greeks, in two late twelfth-century Russian churches, at Staraya Ladoga [110] and at Arkazhy, near Novgorod [111], which show a similar lively linearism. It is difficult to believe that any first-class Greek artist would have left Constantinople to work in Russia. It is possible that we have

110. Saint George. Staraya Ladoga, near Novgorod. *c.* 1167

here again artists representing the provincial school of Thessalonica. On the other hand, the fresco of the Last Judgement in the church of Saint Demetrius at Vladimir, which is of roughly the same date, retains a Classical refinement which suggests that the artist had been well trained at Constantinople

111. Unknown saint. Arkazhy, near Novgorod. *c.* 1189

[112]. But Vladimir was the capital of the Grand Prince of Russia, Vsevolod II, who could well afford to hire an artist from Constantinople specially to adorn his favourite shrine.

11

It is particularly sad that no frescoes of the twelfth century survive in Constantinople; for the fresco was now coming into its own in Byzantine art. Partly this was because the fresco was cheaper and easier to make than the mosaic. The private patrons who now wished to decorate churches could not always afford or obtain the millions of tesserae needed for a whole church, nor the craftsmen to set them. Only the Imperial Court could indulge in such luxuries. But the fresco also fitted the taste of the time. In the old days, when the Empire was the undoubted microcosm of Heaven on earth, the glowing, mysterious splendour of the mosaic was suitable for the Sacred Palace and the shrines of the capital. But now, with growing disillusion and fear, men wanted something more human and intimate. For some time past scenes of Christ's life and of his Mother's on earth had been popular, to illustrate the Liturgy and the Gospels. For such human scenes the fresco-painter had advantages over the mosaic-designer. However fine the cubes might be, the drawing in a mosaic could not be so free as in a fresco; nor could the dyed glass provide such nuances in colour as a palette on which paints could be mixed. Moreover, a mosaic needs perspective and careful optical calculations and lighting. In the small intimate churches that the Byzantines now liked to build the fresco was often more effective.

Fresco-painting had hitherto been mainly a provincial art; and its most remarkable works had been achieved in the rock monasteries of Cappadocia. There the artists had developed a style far removed from the Classical restraint and balance of Imperial art. The drawing was crude and strongly outlined, intended to give a direct emotional effect. Something of the style was now adopted by the fresco-painters of Constantinople. The supreme example of their work that survives is to be seen in the tiny church of Nerez, in northern Macedonia, which the local governor, Alexius Comnenus, a prince of the Imperial house, hired a Constantinopolitan painter to decorate in 1164 [113]. Here the powerful flowing outlines of the Cappadocian school are combined with an elegance in drawing and composition which is of the tradition of the capital. What is added

113. The Transfiguration (detail).
Saint Panteleimon, Nerez. Post-1164

is an intensity of feeling that is new to Byzantine art. The finest
of the panels, the Threne, in which the Mother of God bends
over the body of her Son, has a poignancy unequalled in
Byzantine art. It would be hard to find a more moving
representation of sorrow.

Nerez, though supreme, was not unique. In Cyprus, in the
church of Saint Chrysostom, below the castle of Koutsivendi
or Buffavento, which seems to have been a favourite residence
of the governors of the island, there are the remains of similar
frescoes, dating from about the same time or a little later. The
Threne there is of the same design and has much of the same
intensity of feeling; but the drawing is not quite so sure. It is
tempting to guess that the artist was a pupil of the Master of
Nerez. The frescoes at Vladimir are of the same school; but
their emotional content is a little muted in comparison.

At the same time there was a growing taste for the portable
icon, whether in mosaic or painted on a wooden panel. There
had always been such icons in Constantinople, some of them of
great antiquity and revered for their especial holiness. The most
venerable was the icon of the Mother of God of Blachernae, a
portrait said to be painted from the life by Saint Luke himself.
Most of such icons had been hitherto kept in holy shrines; but
some were intended to be hung in private houses or to accom-
pany a general on his campaigns. Now the demand for them
grew. Partly this was because the sanctuary in a church was no
longer, as in early days, a low railing or parapet but a high
screen, an iconostasis, on which, as the name implies, icons
could be placed. At the same time more people seem to have
wanted to possess holy pictures of their own.

The surviving portable icons of the Constantinopolitan art of
the twelfth century show the same feeling as the frescoes. A
Christ in mosaic, now in the National Museum of Florence

114. Pantocrator. Miniature mosaic. Mid twelfth century

[114], a piece of such excellent workmanship that it must have
come from the workshops of the capital, is reminiscent of the
great Christ of Cefalù, but, despite its small size, it is both more

115. Crucifixion. Miniature mosaic. Twelfth century

majestic and more poignant. A Crucifixion, now in Berlin, is even closer to the style of Nerez [115]. The faces of Christ and of Saint John are a mosaic version of the frescoed faces of Nerez, with the same linear treatment and the same pathos. The face of the Mother of God is unfortunately damaged. The artist has the taste of the time for elongation. The Mother of God is preternaturally tall, as at Torcello; the arms of Christ are preternaturally long. But the drawing within its convention is superb.

The most important, historically as well as artistically, of the portable icons of the twelfth century is the panel painting known as Our Lady of Vladimir [116]. Though parts of it have

116. Our Lady of Vladimir. *c.* 1130

been repainted and though some modern scholars claim that none of the work is earlier than the thirteenth century, the original icon having been burnt in the great fire at Vladimir in 1185, it seems certain that the faces of Our Lady and the Christ-Child are original twelfth-century work. It was probably painted in about 1130 and sent as a gift to Kiev from Constantinople in 1131. In 1155 it was moved to Vladimir, where it soon became famous for its miraculous powers. In style it has the same simple sureness of line as the frescoes at Nerez, and the same human poignancy. It marks the beginning of a new treatment of the Mother of God. Hitherto, whether she was depicted standing alone with her hands uplifted in prayer, as in the holy icon of Blachernae, reputed to be a portrait from the life painted by Saint Luke, or whether she was seated enthroned with the Christ-Child on her knees, as in the great mosaic over the south door of Saint Sophia, or whether she stood with the Christ-Child resting on her left arm while her right hand pointed delicately to him, to show that she is Hodegetria, the Way (the type that was now most usually followed), her head was held erect and her eyes were fixed on the onlooker. Here her head bends sideways, protectively and almost sentimentally, over her Son, and though she is glancing at the onlookers it seems that she has only momentarily raised her eyes from gazing at him. The Child is no longer held at a distance but is pressed lovingly against his Mother's face. The type, known as the Eleousa, the Lady of Compassion, was to be developed later. This is the first appearance of it that has survived. The taste of the time demanded that the Mother of God should be a human mother.

The new importance of the fresco and the panel picture began to bring about a change in the status of the artist. The mosaic had its master-designer, but the work was carried out by numbers of craftsmen. The fresco-painter could design and execute his own work, as the panel-painter inevitably did. Each could therefore command a higher price; and each was more independent, and readier in consequence to receive and experiment with new ideas. A workshop is naturally conservative. In the minor arts, in ivory-carving, which was becoming more infrequent owing to the cost of ivory, and in metal-work, the influence of the new taste, though discernible, was slight. Such crafts depended upon expensive raw materials; and only the Imperial workshops could afford to produce them. Illustrated manuscripts similarly show only faint signs of the new style.

117. Saint John the Baptist, with Saints Philip, Stephen, Andrew and Thomas. Late eleventh or twelfth century

118. Church of the Holy Apostles.
From the Homilies of James of Kokkinobaphos. Early twelfth century

Religious works were for the most part illuminated in the monasteries, where new ideas penetrated slowly. But, as in the church buildings, there was a desire for fewer isolated figures and for many more scenes that illustrated episodes. There is one manuscript at least, illustrating the Homilies of the Monk James of Kokkinobaphos [118], in which the artist in his busy emotional scenes has something of the spirit of the frescoes of Nerez. Secular manuscripts, most of them illustrating Classical works, remained faithful to the Classical style handed down from Hellenistic times.

III

Byzantine civilization in the Comnenian period was a strange mixture of splendour and insecurity, of high sophistication and deep emotionalism. The Byzantines were forced to become conscious of the outside world, particularly of the Westerners who passed insolently through their territory on their way to the Crusades. Between them and the Westerners there was growing suspicion and dislike, worsened by religious controversy. But they were not uninterested in Western ways. The splendid Emperor Manuel I, whose reign lasted from 1141 to 1180, himself the son of a Hungarian princess and the husband first of a German princess and then of a French princess from the Latin East, was fascinated by Western fashions and recreations. But the average citizen of the Empire, who suffered periodically from the ravages of Crusader armies, and who perpetually resented the exploitation of arrogant and avaricious merchants from the Italian maritime cities, to whom in past hours of need the Emperors had given advantageous trading concessions, became increasingly hostile to the West and increasingly apprehensive of its ambitions. When an opportunity occurred, in 1182, the populace of Constantinople enthusiastically pillaged the Italian offices and warehouses in the city and massacred a number of Westerners. It was partly in a spirit of vengeance and partly to exclude their Italian rivals from the rich trade of the Bosphorus and the Black Sea that twenty years later the Venetians persuaded a large Crusading army which was heavily in debt to them to divert its route and attack Constantinople. The Crusaders perhaps genuinely believed that the control of Constantinople would help the general strategy of the Crusades; they were certainly eager to sack a city with such fantastic treasures. As the Venetians were well aware, the Empire had for the last few years been ineptly governed by the incompetent Emperors of the house of Angelus. The Emperor Alexius III did nothing to defend his Empire. The allied Veneto-Crusading expedition arrived off Constantinople in 1203. After some months of negotiation and intrigue, the Crusaders decided in April to take the city by storm. An assault over the sea-walls, aided by treachery in the rear, was successful; and Constantinople was given over to plunder.

We cannot now tell how many works of art perished. The chroniclers speak of libraries being burnt with all their contents. We know that the great silver iconostasis in Saint Sophia was hacked to pieces by the Crusader soldiery. Any precious object that was too big for a man to carry was broken up. Houses and churches were stripped, and mosaics and frescoes that could not be transported were wilfully destroyed. The Venetians, with their finer sense of the value of works of art, looked carefully after their loot and transported it to Venice to adorn their piazzas and their treasuries [119]. Most of the fine examples of Byzantine art that are now to be seen in Venice are goods stolen on this occasion. Amongst the Westerners there were a few men, mostly ecclesiastics, who preserved and made off with holy relics. But it was the sanctity of the relic, not the beauty of its setting, which attracted them. The biographer of the Abbot of Pairis says admiringly of his hero that in his piety he stole only sacred objects.

The sack of Constantinople in 1204 provides the main reason for the survival of so little of the Imperial art of the twelfth century. The lack of evidence is particularly to be regretted, as the century was not only one in which Byzantine taste and the conception of life underlying the taste was changing, but it was also an age of great artistic missionary enterprise stemming from the capital. The Greek artists who worked in Sicily had their pupils; but the school that they founded did not survive the turmoil that followed the end of the Norman dynasty. In Venice the basic Byzantine taste and technique gradually became occidentalized, as can be seen, as far as repairs and restoration permit, in the successive series of mosaics in Saint Mark's. But the Balkan states, Bulgaria and Serbia, were bursting into new activity. They threw off the Byzantine yoke at the end of the twelfth century; and their rulers were eager to patronize the arts and seem to have given protection to Greek artists who had been ruined at the sack of Constantinople or found no employment under its new Latin masters.

119. The Entry into Jerusalem. Enamelled silver-gilt plaque. Twelfth century

120. Tsar Constantine Asen of Bulgaria. Boiana. 1259

In Bulgaria the most important paintings to survive from the thirteenth century are those in the church at Boiana, dating from 1259 [120]. Here the artists, though probably native, had undoubtedly been trained by artists who belonged to the Constantinopolitan school. The work is in a close relationship with the frescoes at Vladimir, humanist and anecdotal, but with a certain Classical restraint. In Serbia the model seems, rather, to have been the near-by church of Nerez and the more poignant school of the twelfth century. At Mileševa, founded by the Serbian king Vladislav about 1235, the frescoes are charged with emotion, expressed in strong brush strokes [121]; but the almost unbearable pathos of Nerez is controlled by the Serbian artists, probably trained by artists from Constantinople or, more particularly, Thessalonica. The Mileševa artists are more naturalistic in their humanism. Their draperies are realistically drawn, and the figures stand firmly, almost too solidly, on the ground. At the church of Sopoćani, painted some thirty years later, the Serbian school reached its height [122]. The figures are still solid, but with the dignified solidity of Classical statuary. The iconography is growing more complicated, but the composition is well controlled; and the whole is still infused with an emotional intensity. The style lasted till the Serbian kingdom itself collapsed before the onslaught of the Turks. But the frescoes of the fourteenth century, of which those at Gračanica are the finest, though magnificent in their general effect, have lost something of the freshness of the earlier work. The style is becoming academic, in response to the Imperial ambitions of the Serbian rulers.

On Russia the influence of Byzantine twelfth-century art was equally remarkable but took a different course. The native Russian artist has never been much interested in Classical restraint. The sober tradition in Byzantine art which was expressed in the frescoes at Vladimir was not followed. But few single pictures can have had so much effect on the art of a whole country as did the icon of Our Lady of Vladimir. It is the ancestor of all the great Russian icons of the Mother of God, in technique as well as in content. The humanism that the Russians learnt from Byzantium was not an interest in the human form, such as was to affect the Serbian school, but an interest in human emotions. The greatest of Russian artists, such as Andrei Rublev, who lived between 1370 and 1430, showed a sense of balanced composition that was in its way

121 (*above*). King Vladislav I of Serbia. Mileševa. *c*. 1235

122. Group of Apostles, detail from a Koimisis. Sopoćani. *c*. 1265

123. Abraham and the Angels at Mamre
(or the Old Testament Trinity). Attributed to Andrei Rublev. *c.* 1410

Classical [123]; but in general Russian art preferred its own
type of fantasy, without ever forgetting its roots in twelfth-
century Byzantium.

Meanwhile the art of Constantinople itself moved on to its
final age of glory.

6

The Last Splendour

The Crusaders' capture of Constantinople was a blow from which the Empire could never fully recover; but it was not the end of the Byzantine world. The conquerors carved out the Imperial territories between themselves without waiting to conquer them all. Their conquests were large. A Latin Emperor was set up in Constantinople and controlled the neighbouring lands on both sides of the Straits. Frankish knights captured Thessalonica and successfully invaded the Greek peninsula. The Venetians prudently concentrated on islands and sea-ports that would be of value to their trade. But in Epirus, in north-west Greece, members of the fallen Angelus dynasty founded a Despotate which soon spread its dominion into Macedonia and in 1224 re-took Thessalonica for the Greeks. Further to the east scions of the Comnenian family set up an empire at Trebizond which was to last till 1461, seven years after the Turkish conquest of Constantinople. The Grand Comnenus of Trebizond soon became a wealthy potentate, not only because he owned silver mines in the neighbouring hills but still more because his capital lay at the end of the great trade-route that ran from the Far East through northern Persia, a route that became especially active with the establishment of the Mongol Empire in the mid thirteenth century. Nearer to Constantinople Theodore Lascaris, son-in-law of the Emperor Alexius III, rallied the leading exiles from the capital in the ancient city of Nicaea, where he soon proclaimed himself as Emperor and appointed a Patriarch for the Church of the Empire. To the majority of the Greeks the Emperor and Patriarch at Nicaea represented legitimacy.

Theodore I Lascaris and his son-in-law and successor, John III Vatatzes, were administrators of high ability, while John's son Theodore II was, though less practical, a distinguished scholar. Under their rule the Nicaean Empire prospered, driving the Westerners out of Asia and then gradually reconquering the European provinces. The annexation of Thessalonica in 1246 put an end to the rival claims of the Despots of Epirus. Meanwhile, though in Greece itself the Frankish principalities lasted on for several generations, some in Central Greece, such as the Duchy of Athens, passing straight from Frankish to Turkish rule, and the Peloponnese was only wholly reoccupied in the early fifteenth century, the Latin Empire of 'Romania' tottered impoverished to its fall. In 1261 the Nicaean Emperor Michael VIII Palaeologus, regent and co-Emperor for Theodore II's young son John IV, recovered Constantinople; and the Empire was re-established in its old capital.

The artists and architects scattered by the Frankish conquest had thus a number of courts in which they could take refuge. Some must have stayed on in the conquered capital. The Latin rulers had little use for Byzantine builders and decorators. In Constantinople they seem to have built very little. Instead, they dismantled and destroyed. In his poverty the Latin Emperor Baldwin II removed and sold the leaden roofs from the halls of the old Imperial Palace and dispersed most of what was left of the great Imperial collection of relics, which were bought from dealers by Saint Louis of France, who built the Sainte Chapelle in Paris to house them. In the conquered provinces the Frankish princes preferred to introduce the Gothic style that they knew at home. Only one branch of art continued uninterrupted in Constantinople throughout the Latin Empire. There were still workshops in the city where manuscripts were copied and illustrated, attached to Greek monasteries that the Latins did not venture to close, and to which some of the Court miniaturists may have retired. There exist some illustrated Gospels which undoubtedly belong to the earlier thirteenth century and in which the introduction of Latin texts in the pictures suggests that they were designed or amended for Frankish patrons [124]. They are in the old Metropolitan tradition, showing the signs of the times only in a certain broadening of the figures and, in contrast, tapering legs and an increased delicacy in the folds of the garments.

The rulers of the Greek succession states were eager to carry out the traditional duty of an Emperor in patronizing the arts. The Despots of Epirus were indefatigable in building churches, nearly all of them small, as was now the fashion in Byzantine circles, though at their capital, Arta, the buildings were more impressive. Of their palace nothing survives; and the principal church, the Paregoritissa, is, it must be confessed, a clumsy and

124. Saint John the Evangelist.
From a Gospel made for a Frankish patron. *c.* 1250

125. Church of the Paregoritissa at Arta. 1282–9

provincial piece of work [125]. From the outside it looks like a
box with handles on top. The inside seems to be based on the
church of Holy Luke in Styris, built over two centuries earlier,
with the central dome resting on squinches. But the treatment
of the squinches, with four tiers of rows of thin columns, looks
inappropriately Gothic, while the hard horizontal lines of the
roof add to the box-like effect. The central dome contains a
mosaic Pantocrator, with a circle of prophets and saints
beneath him. The Pantocrator has a kinship to Sicilian work,
while the prophets and saints seem to hark back to the style of
the Nea Moni mosaics. One has the impression that the best
Byzantine artists did not bother to go to Arta. Other churches
in Arta and in towns that were under Epirot influence, such as
Castoria, were almost all of them tiny basilicas, some with only
wooden roofs, though from the thirteenth century onwards
vaults and a central dome were usually introduced. Some older

168

churches, such as Saint Demetrius at Arta, were provided by the Despots with a new vaulted roof and a dome. There was a tendency now to elaborate the exterior with ornamental brick-work, a fashion that may have been introduced from Norman Sicily. It was to be a popular fashion in the Byzantine provinces, as the fourteenth-century churches at Mesemvria on the Black Sea coast bear witness.

Epirot art was provincial. It was in the richer capitals of Nicaea and Trebizond that metropolitan art was continued. There is little now left of the art of Nicaea. The city itself has suffered too much destruction; and in the second capital of the Empire, Magnesia, nothing has survived. The holiest shrine in Nicaea, the Church of the Dormition, had been decorated with mosaics in the eleventh century, mosaics which perished in 1922. The Nicaean Emperors seem to have added nothing there. But the Metropolitan Church of Saint Sophia was re-decorated with frescoes, a few traces of which survive. The Nicaean Emperors, though they were great patrons of scholar-ship, were thrifty folk who did not indulge in extravagant artistic programmes. The Emperor John Vatatzes only allowed his Empress a new crown when sufficient money had been made from the Palace poultry-farm to pay for it.

The court of the Grand Comnenus was more lavish. It is at Trebizond that, in spite of the destructive hand of time and the infidel, we can see new trends in art emerging. Neither Nicaea nor Trebizond seems to have contributed anything in architecture that was untraditional; and though old travellers speak of mosaics in the Church of the Panagia Chrysokephalos, no mosaic work now exists in the city. It is possible that there were never large enough glass-factories to permit of mosaic decoration; but Trapezuntine taste clearly favoured frescoes. This was almost certainly because the fresco offered the possibility of a greater and subtler variation in colouring. It is in thirteenth-century work at Trebizond that we first find a new range of colours. The more linear style of Comnenian art is abandoned. Highlights in dead white or in bright colours pro-vide the modelling outlines. Elsewhere the gradations are delicate. With the new palette there comes what seems to be a deliberate disregard for realism. We begin to have scarlet horses and green oxen, vermilion and yellow houses and walls and chocolate-coloured foliage. These fanciful tints did not have any symbolic meaning. Rather, the artist, who conceived

126A. Jacob and the Angel. Saint Sophia, Trebizond. *c.* 1260

composition in terms of colour, used his pigments to provide emphasis in the picture; and as holy figures had their traditional colouring, other objects could be coloured to suit the composition.

After the Greek recovery of Constantinople the intellectuals of Trebizond paid frequent visits to the old Imperial capital and often settled there; and Trapezuntine painters no doubt followed in their wake, bringing their ideas with them. In Russia and the Danubian principalities in the fourteenth and early fifteenth centuries Trebizond seems to have had a more powerful artistic influence than Constantinople itself.

126B. Annunciation. Narthex, Saint Sophia, Trebizond. c. 1250

The re-establishment of the Empire in the great Imperial city
brought new hope and confidence to the Byzantines. It was true
that the Emperor was no longer the one great Oecumenical
Orthodox monarch. He had Orthodox neighbours, the Kings
of Bulgaria and Serbia, whose territories were now larger and
richer than his own; and away to the north the Grand Prince
of Russia was soon to outclass them all. But as Emperor of
New Rome he commanded a special prestige; his recognition
and approval meant much to the quarrelling Balkan princes.
It was true that Constantinople itself, after the disastrous Latin
occupation, was a city of ruins and empty spaces. But the trade-
routes that the Mongol conquest of Asia was beginning to
organize brought new wealth through Trebizond and other
Black Sea ports to the markets of Constantinople. Though the
Italians had captured the carrying trade and could insist on
having their new colonies on the Golden Horn, the Genoese
across the water at Pera, the Venetians, a little later, within
Constantinople itself, yet it was in the bazaars of the old city

that the merchandise was mainly exchanged. Money poured into the city, to the benefit of the bazaar-keepers and the officials who controlled the excise and the monopolies. It was still possible to be very rich in Byzantium.

The euphoria induced by the recovery of the capital did not last for long. The victorious Emperor Michael Palaeologus was faced by dangerous foreign problems, with Western powers eager for revenge; and his attempt to buy them off by offering to bring his Church under the authority of Rome infuriated the vast majority of the clergy and the people, who were already shocked by his ruthless and unscrupulous treatment of the young Emperor whose throne he had usurped and whose person he had solemnly sworn to protect. The Empire was saved by the great conspiracy which culminated in the massacre of the Sicilian Vespers and ruined his chief enemy, Charles of Anjou, King of Sicily. It had been for the Emperor an expensive conspiracy; much of the treasure accumulated by the thrift of the Nicaean Emperors was used up. Meanwhile the administration and victualling of Constantinople added to the expenses of

127 (*opposite*). The Prophet Elijah. Fresco in the church at Gračanica. 1321

128. The church at Gračanica. 1321

173

129. The Grand Logothete Theodore Metochites. *c.* 1315–21

the government. Soon the Emperors found themselves poorer than some of their subjects, particularly the nobility who owned town property or large country estates and ministers who were paid for their services by the gift of the control of customs-dues or monopolies.

Michael VIII's son and heir, Andronicus II, was an amiable, pious and cultured man whose two chief ministers, Nicephorus Chumnus and Theodore Metochites [129], were even finer scholars; but all three were useless as administrators. The Empire was dangerously threatened by the growing Balkan kingdoms and, more ominously, by a vigorous Turkish emirate that had sprung up in Western Anatolia, under Osman and his Ottoman successors; and the Empire proved powerless to prevent their advance into its territory. In 1328 Andronicus II was dethroned after some years of civil war by his grandson, Andronicus III, who was a more vigorous but scarcely a more successful ruler. He died in 1341; and the fifty years' reign of his son, John V, was a period of unmitigated disaster. There were civil wars; John was thrice deposed from power, by his father-in-law, his eldest son and his grandson, though he died on the throne. There were ghastly visitations of the plague; the Black Death in 1346 killed probably a third of the population of Constantinople. At one time it seemed that the Serbian King, Stephen Dushan, might absorb the whole Empire; but it was the Ottoman Turks who were its more deadly enemies. When John V died he was the vassal of the Ottoman Sultan, whose territories entirely surrounded his few remaining possessions, Constantinople, Thessalonica, and a few coastal towns and islands. Only in the Peloponnese, where cadets of the Imperial house ruled as Despots of the Morea from their little capital of Mistra, did Byzantine arms and diplomacy enjoy any success. Money was running short. The Mongol Empire was disintegrating and less trade was coming through the Black Sea to the Bosphorus. John V's second son and ultimate successor, Manuel II, the most attractive and civilized Emperor to rule in Byzantium, could do little to stop the decline. His eldest son, John VIII, tried by uniting his Church with Rome to involve the West in the defence of Constantinople. But the West would not, nor really could, send adequate aid; and John's subjects angrily repudiated his policy of union. The city was preserved merely because the Sultan, Murad II, was a comparatively peaceable man. When a brilliant and vigorous Sultan, Mehmet II, ascended the Ottoman throne, Constantinople was doomed. John's brother, Constantine XI, led his people in a gallant but hopeless struggle to defend the Empire. On 29 May 1453, all was over. Byzantium was no more.

III

Against this background of foreign invasion and civil war, of plague and poverty, there flourished in Constantinople a civilization more brilliant than any that Byzantium had known before. The population might be diminishing and dwindling away, but never before had there been in Constantinople so many erudite scholars and inquiring scientists. If few of their works can be read with pleasure today, the same is true of most of the writers of the Italian Renaissance. But though their literary style was all too often appallingly intricate and long-winded, that was the fashion of the time. Their minds were active and acute. It is difficult to explain how in an atmosphere of decadence and deepening depression such liveliness could flourish. But culture has little to do with political stability; and these latter Byzantines were conscious that they possessed one huge asset: they were Greeks. The Empire had shrunk to territories that had been Greek since the dawn of civilization. Its inhabitants were geographically, if not racially, Greeks. As Greeks they had something to offer to the world. In the thirteenth century Western Europe began to learn of the importance of ancient Greek culture from Arabic intermediaries. Then, partly as the result of the Latin occupation which brought Westerners to live in Greek lands, and partly as a result of Papal efforts to secure the submission of the Greek Church, which involved the use of missionaries trained to understand the Greeks, the West began to realize that in Byzantium Classical lore was studied in its original tongue. Much as it despised the Greeks politically and disliked them religiously, it began to respect them intellectually. On their side the Greeks, with their characteristic mixture of great ideas and practical common-sense, while they still insisted that they were Romans, the heirs of the Roman Empire, began to speak of themselves as Hellenes, using a term that in earlier Byzantine days was, except when applied to language, used for heathens as opposed to Christian Greeks.

The same vigour and the same pride in the Classical past shone in the art of the Palaeologan period. The art of the great Imperial centuries had been Classical in its proportion and its restraint; but now it was, rather, the crowded humanist art of the Hellenistic age that provided the model. The tense emotion that had been visible in the twelfth century was discarded. The Palaeologan artists were ready to depict pain and sorrow as well as serenity and bliss, but they did so as story-tellers. In the churches they were even more intent than their predecessors on illustrating the Liturgy. The single figures of the saints are there in their proper places; but the saints are seen as human beings illumined with grace. The artists are more particularly interested in depicting whole episodes in the life of Christ and of his Mother. The scene necessarily forms a picture in itself, but it is still part of the whole decorative liturgical scheme of the building. This affects the composition of each scene and involves a certain compromise. The scene often has to show a sequence of events that make up a whole episode. The Nativity, for example, has to include the recumbent Mother, the Baby in the crib and the Baby's ceremonial bath, as well as the angels appearing to the shepherds [130]. The eye therefore should not attempt to see it all at once as a whole but as in the old days should travel round it. Consequently the perspective is not always unified, and varying types of perspective are used. Sometimes figures seem almost to be tumbling out of the bottom of the picture space, and sometimes the space is enlarged by carrying the scene on into side-niches, set at a slight angle to the main picture.

130. The Nativity. The church of Christ in Chora, Constantinople

The style is humanistic, but not realistic in the modern sense. The realism is, on the contrary, Platonic. These liturgical scenes were to be intelligible to the ordinary worshipper, but at the same time they suggested the real world of which the pictorial representation was the shadow. If the colouring was often fanciful by natural standards, that was because visible nature was only a transient copy of incorporeal reality. For practical purposes the depicted object should be recognizable. Its form should reproduce the eternal prototype. But colour, being light, should conform to the divine harmony of colours. It was the fresco-painters who indulged in the most intense and fantastic colouring. The mosaicists, working in a naturally more luminous material, were less adventurous.

The iconographical conventions of the past remained in force. The main outlines of the scheme of church-decoration were unaltered, with minor local variations, while side-chapels might have their own individual scheme. The profile was still generally avoided except for such evil figures as the Devil in scenes of the Temptation, or King Herod or the soldiers who massacre the Innocents. But the rule is slightly relaxed. Already in the twelfth century subsidiary figures in a scene, hand-maidens or onlookers, might be shown in profile. In the fourteenth century we find the sick healed by Christ sometimes shown in profile, and even Saint Joseph himself, as though to show that he was but an earthly bridegroom. The portraits of donors attempt to be actual portraits, carrying on the fashion started in the twelfth century. The artist attempts to catch the individual spirit of his sitter, as was recommended in the Neoplatonist writings which were now read and admired by the intellectuals of the time. It must be confessed that usually, and especially with the painters of illuminated manuscripts, always the most conservative among Byzantine artists, while the faces are portraits, the robes are stiff and conventional. But throughout, in spite of the surviving conventions, the art of the Palaeologan period shows more ease, more movement and a greater desire to please aesthetically than the art of any other period of Byzantine history.

This style is curiously out of keeping with the sombre political and economic background of the time. But it must be remembered that its chief surviving monuments in Constantinople and in Thessalonica date from the early fourteenth century, before the political decadence of the Empire was fully realized. The inhabitants of Constantinople were always inclined to ignore what was happening in the provinces. There was still great wealth in the city and in Thessalonica. Though the Ottoman Turks were already advancing in Anatolia, the significance of their advance was as yet unnoticed at Constantinople. The Thessalonians should perhaps have been alarmed by the growing power of the Serbian kingdom; but as yet they were only conscious that the new wealth in the Balkans meant more business for their markets. The artists of the time had no particular reason to believe that they were living in a decadent age. The Neoplatonic basis of all Byzantine art kept them aware that they were only depicting the shadow of reality. But it was not now a sombre shadow. They were fortified by an intensified study of the works of their Classical, and especially their Hellenistic, ancestors. They intended their pictures to represent eternal truths, but they intended them also to please.

It was not, however, an Imperial art, nor did it show the touch of anguish apparent in the twelfth century, when the old Imperial ideal was breaking down. By the beginning of the fourteenth century the Imperial Court was no longer the chief patron of the arts. The Imperial workshops do not seem to have been reconstituted after the recovery of Constantinople. The Emperor could no longer afford them. He had less money to spare for the arts than had several of his subjects. The foundation, rehabilitation and decoration of churches and monasteries were now carried out under the patronage of individual magnates, of rich ladies connected with the Imperial family, such as Andronicus II's first cousin, Theodora Palaeologaena, and her descendants, who redecorated the Church of Our Lady of Sure Hope, or Maria, Lady of the Mongols, bastard daughter of Michael VIII, widow of the Tartan Ilkhan of Persia, who founded the church known as Mary of the Mongols and had a hand in the endowment of Our Saviour in Chora, the general Michael Tarchionites Glabas who redecorated the church of the Pammakaristos and built its exquisite funerary chapel, the statesman Nicephorus Chumnus, who redecorated Our Lady of Swift Succour, and his rival Theodore Metochites, to whom the superb work in Our Saviour in Chora is primarily due. At Thessalonica the early fourteenth-century church of the Holy Apostles was built and decorated at his own expense by the Metropolitan of the city, Niphon, later Patriarch of Constantinople.

Each of these patrons was, in the Greek phrase, the 'poetic' cause of the work that he commissioned; and the work presumably reflected his personal tastes. If the mosaics in the chapel of the Pammakaristos seem soft and almost over-pretty in comparison with the contemporary work in the church of the Chora, this was doubtless because the retired general Michael Glabas had the rather sentimental tastes often to be found in army officers, whereas Theodore Metochites was a philosopher steeped in ancient Greek learning, eager that the work that he patronized should be as Classical as possible. The actual artists were still anonymous; but it is probable that their status was rising. They were no longer minor government servants working under the orders of the Imperial bureaucracy. They were now free artisans whose services the patrons of the time had to hire. The mosaicists must have worked as a team; it would have been difficult for an artist to undertake a large panel by himself. But there was probably one master artist controlling the decoration. Though it was his business to carry out his patron's wishes, the designer of a decorative scheme such as that of the mosaics in the church of the Chora must have been a highly responsible man of great technical and artistic knowledge. Fresco panels, on the other hand, were necessarily the work of a single artist, who both sketched in the design on the plaster and applied the paint. He had to combine artistic with technical skill, and was therefore a person of consequence who was beginning to want personal recognition and, therefore, to sign his work. But he was necessarily subservient to his patron, as he could not produce his work unless there was someone to pay for it. The artist who was the first to obtain personal recognition was the individual icon-painter. He did not necessarily have to wait for a patron. If he were good there would be numerous clients for his works. Nevertheless, though in Russia artists such as Rublev and Theophanes the Greek were known by name by the end of the fourteenth century, it was not till after the fall of Constantinople that the names of individual Greek artists working in Greek lands began to be distinguished. With the decline of the 'poetic' cause of the work of art the 'organic' cause became more important.

Of the works of art that still survive from the early Palaeologan period by far the most splendid is the decoration of the church of Saint Saviour in Chora, the present Kahriye Cami [131, 132]. There may have been other works as magnificent. It is curious that no foreign traveller visiting Constanti-

nople in the fourteenth or fifteenth century makes any mention of the church, though there is praise for mosaics in the church of the Pantocrator or of Saint John in Petra. This may be because it contained at the time no particularly venerable relic and therefore was not on the regular pilgrim's itinerary. The philosopher-statesman, Theodore Metochites, who was responsible for the decoration, had no doubts of its importance, and his pupil, the historian Gregoras, regarded it as a great achievement. Certainly it remains today a supreme example of late Byzantine art. The mosaics are remarkable for the technical skill with which the material is used to satisfy the tastes of the time, In the old Imperial mosaics movement was provided by the play of light upon the cubes, but the majestic figures themselves were super-human and serene. In the Chora, though the individual figures of Christ and the saints still keep something of the shimmering dignity of the past, their faces and their gestures are humanized; and in the group-scenes faces, gestures and poses are all planned to stress the human story, and, above all, there is movement in the drawing. In some of the scenes there is, perhaps, too much movement for the medium; mosaic is not really suitable to depict such liveliness. It is when we pass to the frescoes in the side-chapel that we see Palaeologan art at its most remarkable. The synthesis there is complete, There is a rich new range of colour, used with splendour and with delicacy to supplement the moulding in the drawing. The drawing and the composition reflect Hellenistic classical traditions, but are vivified by a tremendous feeling for move- ment and are saved from facile humanism by a touch of the intensity of emotion inherited from the twelfth century and from the monks of Cappadocia. The great Anastasis in the apse, with Christ raising Adam and Eve from Hell, surely represents one of the high-water marks in the history of art [133].

It is possible that the frescoes temporarily uncovered in the Church of Saint Euphemia belonged to the same period. They show a similar style and accomplishment though less vitality. But if there were other similar frescoes of the time in Con- stantinople they have perished. The other contemporary

132 (*opposite*). An Angel Rolling Back the Scroll of Heaven, detail from 131

133 (*overleaf*). The Anastasis (detail), in the church of Christ in Chora, Constantinople

mosaics, in the unidentified building now known as the Kilisse Cami and in the church of the Holy Apostles at Thessalonica, are rather too fragmentary to be properly assessed. The background of the former is of white cubes and of the latter blue, perhaps because gold was now too expensive, but perhaps too because it corresponded with the taste of the time. The mosaics in the side-chapel of the Pammakaristos are technically very fine; but they are gently, almost sentimentally, pretty; they lack the vitality of the work in the Chora.

IV

After the 1320s, when the decoration of the church of the Chora and other contemporary buildings was finished, no further major work of art was undertaken in Constantinople. The Empire was weakened and impoverished by civil war and plague and threats from foreign invaders. No one had the money or the energy or confidence to patronize a great enterprise. Minor additions and repairs were made to buildings. In 1346 an earthquake severely damaged the dome and the sanctuary of Saint Sophia, without, however, damaging the mosaics in the apse. The Empress-Regent Anna hastily had the building repaired. We know that the church of Our Lady of Sure Help contained frescoes ordered in the late fourteenth century by the grandchildren of its foundress. Sepulchral ornaments were added to the church of the Chora, the last of which shows traces of a fresco, dating from the fifteenth century, that is quite Italian in style. But when in 1434 one of the holiest shrines in Byzantium, the church of Our Lady of Blachernae, was almost entirely destroyed by fire, no attempt was made to rebuild it. There was too little money left in the city for the task and probably too few craftsmen. The great ceremonies of the Court had long since been curtailed. In the fifteenth century the Burgundian traveller, Bertrandon de la Brocquière, was shocked to see the Empress Maria, a lovely princess from Trebizond, ride to Mass at Saint Sophia with only two ladies, two or three knights and three eunuchs in attendance. She was splendidly dressed and, he thought, used too many cosmetics. Fine costumes were still to be seen in Constantinople, though the Emperor Manuel II preferred to wear robes of chaste but well-laundered white; but the Imperial jewels had for some time been made of coloured glass, and gold and silver plate were giving way to earthenware [134, 135].

134. Saint Eudocia.
Incrustation work set in marble. Tenth century (?)

In Thessalonica, which had been as rich as the capital, the rule of the revolutionary Zealots, from 1342 to 1350, had done irreparable harm to the economy. There too artistic activity on a grand scale ceased: though the little church of the monastery of Vlateon, by the citadel, was built and decorated at the end of the fourteenth century. The magnates of the two great cities

135. Two-masted ship. A Byzantine earthenware plate, found at Corinth. Thirteenth century

could no longer afford to exercise patronage. The artists had to find clients elsewhere.

Minor arts were continued. Small portable mosaic icons were fashionable in the fourteenth century; and though most of those that survive date clearly from its earlier decades [136], there are one or two which for historical reasons can be dated later than 1350. They show in miniature the same Classical humanism as the greater panels. Icons painted on wood were produced in increasing numbers. Many of them were intended for unsophisticated clients and were emotional and a little crude; but the best of them show the high aristocratic quality of the mosaics. Manuscript illumination was continued into the fifteenth century and showed to the last the interest in portraiture characteristic of the time, though garments and back-

136. The Transfiguration. Miniature mosaic.
Late thirteenth or early fourteenth century

137. The Kiss of Judas. Church of Saint Clement, Ohrid. 1295

grounds remain stiff and conventional, and some even of the
Imperial portraits retain the old hieratic flatness.

There was only one part of the Byzantine world which had
not sunk into decay by the later fourteenth century. In the
Peloponnese the Despots of the Morea were extending their
dominion, by arms and by diplomacy, till on the eve of the
Turkish conquest the whole peninsula, with the exception of
two or three Venetian-held sea-ports, was again in Greek
hands. The Morea was fortunate in its Despots, all of them men
of energy and culture who liked to attract scholars and artists
to their Court in the little city of Mistra. In the early years of the
fourteenth century Mistra was renowned for possessing an
academy run by the most remarkable philosopher in all
Byzantine history, George Gemistus Plethon, whose fame was
great even overseas in Italy. The artistic achievements of Mistra
were less internationally renowned; but they represent the last
flowering of Byzantine art. In Constantinople the Palaeologan

138. Saint Merkurios.
Church of Saint Clement, Ohrid. 1295

139. The Crucifixion, with scenes from the Passion.
The Bessarion Reliquary. *c.* 1400

patrons for the most part repaired existing buildings. At Mistra
new churches were built. Many of them followed classical
Byzantine plans, with a cross inscribed in a square and a dome
supported on four pillars. Others, while externally of the same
pattern, with a central dome and four small domes at the four

140. The Emperor John VI Cantacuzenus as a monk.
Detail from a miniature. *c.* 1370

141. Saints Peter, James and John.
Detail from a miniature of the Transfiguration. *c.* 1370

corners, internally were basilicas with three naves, the smaller domes being blind calottes. The brick-work of the exterior was elaborately decorated; the buildings were given a deliberately picturesque grouping; and belfry towers, an innovation inherited from the Franks, were often added. The secular architecture, to judge from the Palace of the Despots and such larger houses as have survived, shows even stronger Western influences, particularly Venetian. Even the Gothic arch is sometimes used.

The same interest in Western art is shown in the secular manuscripts which can be ascribed to the school of Mistra. In earlier times the illustrations of Classical secular works kept to the old Hellenistic tradition, preserving an almost unaltered Classicism, whatever the religious fashions might be. Now such favourite works as Oppian's *Cynegetica* are illustrated with figures in westernized costumes, in positions and groups quite 'ien to the Hellenistic models [142]. Lay life in the Peloponnese

ὁ σὰ κε μὴ θήρησιν ἐπόμματος ὕπνου ἔλοιτο.
ἢ ἐκ βομδίων λιπαροῖς ἐν ποσὶ πεδίλων.
μὴ δ' ἄρα λωπὸς ἔχαν μάλα λώϊον αὐένετο ἔρα
πολλάκι κινυμένοιο πνοιῇ κὴ ἀάδθυλος αὔτω
θήρας ἀν' εἴποίησεν. αὐνίξαν δὲ φέβυ εται.

had been too deeply affected by Frankish rule not to show its reflection.[1]

Religious painting, however, remained closed to Western influence. Dislike of the Western Church, combined with differences in the Liturgy and in the attitude to the Liturgy,

143. Birth of a Monster. From a mid fourteenth-century manuscript of *The Romance of Alexander the Great*

1. A parallel tendency can be seen in a late fourteenth-century Romance of Alexander, now in the Casa dei Greci at Venice, which was almost certainly decorated at Constantinople. In it the Persians all wear contemporary Turkish costumes [143].

made any assimilation of ecclesiastical decoration difficult to achieve. The painters of the frescoes in the churches of Mistra carried on the style that had reached a climax in the church of the Chora. In the two finest of the mid-fourteenth-century Mistra churches, the Aphentico (sometimes called the Bronto-

144. The Brontocheion,
Mistra. *c.* 1300

145. The Mother of God. Fresco in the Church of the Peribleptos,
Mistra. Late fourteenth century

cheion), and the Mother of God Peribleptos [145], there is the
same Classical humanism as in the Chora, but perhaps a little
less vigour and a little more conscious elegance and a touch of
wistfulness. The drawing is delicate and expressive and the
colours glow warmly. In the picture of the Nativity in the
Peribleptos, which is one of the masterpieces of Byzantine art,
there is an added richness and fantasy in the colouring and an
airy lightness in the composition. The figures float rather than
move. Only the humanity of the faces keeps us from passing
into a world of dreams. It was a time when men were beginning
foresee the end of the Empire and foretell the end of the

146. The Raising of Lazarus. Fresco in the Church of the Pantanassa,
Mistra. 1428

world, with Anti-Christ and Armageddon close ahead. The
master-artist of the Peribleptos seems, while still stressing the
humanity of the present, to wish to suggest the beauty of things
in the true reality that is to come.

The Church of the Mother of God Pantanassa was decorated
in the early fifteenth century. The technique of its master-artist
is superbly accomplished. His use of line and of colour makes
this last work of independent Byzantium an achievement of
supreme beauty. But the atmosphere of wistfulness is stronger,
and there is a certain miniature quality, as though a painter
trained to practise the delicate detailed style of an illuminatio

was transferring his style to a larger area without adequately altering its scale. There is nothing monumental left now in Byzantine art. At the petty but civilized Court of the Despots of Mistra a monumental conception would have been out of place. The Empire was dying. It was not surprising that its art should be reaching a dead end.

Late Byzantine artists have often been condemned for a failure to 'progress'; and the blame has often been laid upon the triumph of Hesychasm, the quietist movement within the Byzantine Church. But, rightly or wrongly, the Byzantine religious artist did not wish to progress along Western lines. His role, as he saw it, was to complement the Liturgy. It was to show the earthly shadow of the Divine Presence within the holy building. He was dealing with eternal things that do not change. Within the limits of his purpose he was ready to experiment with new techniques and even new symbols. If the art of the frescoes at Mistra represents the closing of a chapter, that was due to political circumstances. The Turkish conquest meant that there could be no more of the patronage by culti-vated magnates which had been the 'poetic' cause of the great works of art of the fourteenth century. For the future patronage could only be provided by a hampered and impoverished Church, or by merchants belonging to a subject race for whom any display of wealth would probably entail imprisonment and death.

7
Conclusion

I

Greek ecclesiastical art lasted on beyond the fall of Constantinople. But it would no longer be correct to call it
Byzantine art. To the Byzantines the 'poetic' cause of art, the
patronage, had been the active generating force. Deprived of
the Imperial Court, with its cultured princes and princesses and
its highly educated civil service, and, most of all, deprived of
its Emperor, the sacred, if often unworthy, representative of
God on earth, Byzantium lost the basis of its political philosophy. An infidel Sultan sitting on the throne of the Caesars
could not represent the Christian God. The Greeks were
permitted to remain as a nation, a second-class nation, under
their Turkish overlord, who entrusted their administration to
the head of their Church organization, the Patriarch of Constantinople. But the Patriarch, though he inherited something
of the functions of the Emperor, could not inherit his mystical
prestige. He did his best. He strove to keep at least the standards
of education from shrinking too low. But, harassed by his alien
masters, his tenure of office dependent on their whim, his own
subordinates too often dominated by the spirit of intrigue to
which second-class nations are prone, and his own material
resources dwindling and uncertain, he could barely maintain
his ecclesiastical organization and his schools. There was no
money left for the patronage of the arts. After a few decades a
class of rich Greek merchants emerged; but their fortunes and
even their lives were always in danger, from the jealousy that
their wealth aroused among their Turkish overlords. Their
patronage was necessarily limited. The older Christian churches
in Constantinople and other big cities were annexed one by one
by Sultans and viziers; and permission to build a new church
was only granted if the building was unostentatious and humble
and there were no external evidence of a dome. Under such
circumstances no patronage could be expected from the
Patriarchal Court.

A. Church of the Annunciation at Vatra Moldovitsa, Moldavia. 1532

Except for the Tsar of Russia, in whose distant territories a national neo-Byzantine art had already developed, and for the Kings of Georgia, who were now almost entirely isolated from the rest of Christendom, the only Orthodox rulers left in the world were the Princes of Wallachia and Moldavia, vassals to the Sultan but autonomous within their dominions. They did their best to carry on the tradition of royal patronage. They built and decorated churches and monasteries, they encouraged icon-painting and the illuminating of manuscripts, as well as the minor arts of metal-work and figured textiles. In Wallachia architects and artists followed traditional Byzantine styles; but none of them were distinguished in design or technique. In Moldavia, especially in the north of the principality, a more individual style developed of churches with high gabled roofs and domes hidden in small conical towers, intended to bear the heavy winter snows, fully frescoed not only inside but on the outside walls also, under the broad sheltering eaves [147A, B]. The result is often lively and charming; but it is a provincial art. The craftsmen in the minor arts, working under the direct patronage of the Princes, were more accomplished and carried on not unworthily the traditions of Constantinople. Later,

147B. Church of the Annunciation at Vatra Moldovitsa, Moldavia. 1532

when the Greeks of Constantinople learnt how to amass riches even under Turkish rule, they began to invest their wealth in the autonomous Principalities. Before the close of the seventeenth century they had become by intermarriage or by purchase the chief land-owners in the Principalities; and throughout the eighteenth century their scions sat upon the Princely thrones. They were eager patrons, especially of architecture. But as they were determined to maintain and emphasize a connection with Western Christendom, they liked to import architects from Italy, who produced for them a style that is a not unsuccessful merging of Venetian baroque with the Byzantine tradition. Indeed, if we wish to see how Byzantine architecture would probably have developed had the Empire endured, it is to the churches and palaces in Bucharest and Jassy and their environs that we must look. The Princes took a far slighter interest in painting. The Orthodox ecclesiastical authorities had no objection to an alien architect; but the church paintings were part of their liturgy; they would not allow heretic painters to interfere there. The Princes' western protégés were not welcome inside the churches, so the Princes restricted their patronage of painting to commissioning portraits of themselves and their families.

Elsewhere in the Greek world it was the Church that kept painting alive. There was always work for artists in the great monastic republic of Mount Athos. Churches and refectories and libraries were always being built and rebuilt, decorated and redecorated on the Mountain; and many of the most accomplished Greek artists of the sixteenth century went to work there; but by the seventeenth century the Mountain was poorer and was growing more static. It preferred to employ its own monastic artists, men whose training was narrow and who remained all too faithful to tradition. The same sequence can be found in smaller monastic communities, such as the monasteries on the rocks of Meteora in Thessaly, and in small towns in northern Greece, where the Turkish authorities did not trouble to restrict the building of churches. There too it seems that at first itinerant professional artists were employed, but later the monk-artist from the nearest monastery would be brought in to do the work. In Crete, which the Venetians held until the seventeenth century, there was greater activity. Though the Venetians tried to impose the authority of Rome on the Orthodox in the island and continually interfered in the administration of their church, they did not put any restriction

148. Dionysiou Monastery,
Mount Athos. Paintings in the refectory. Sixteenth century

upon the building and decoration of churches, nor did they prevent their subjects from travelling. Cretan artists were therefore usually more lively and less rigid than their fellows on the mainland. But they suffered from the lack of wealthy patronage. The Cretan Church was poor. Many of them had to go to Mount Athos or to the richer towns of northern Greece in order to find work. Others went to Venice, where patrons abounded. But if they went there they had to adapt their art to Venetian taste; and very few were able to do so with success. However, amongst those few was Dominico Theotocopulo, surnamed El Greco, through whom something of the Byzantine feeling for composition and for colour and light was transmitted to Spain and the West.

In the Ionian Islands, where the Greeks were more closely integrated with their Venetian masters and where there was curiously little enmity between the Orthodox and Catholic Churches, a bastard Greco-Venetian art developed which was never very satisfactory: though some of its products have a certain pleasing charm.

The decline of the patron meant the enhancement of the individual artist. Inscriptions no longer celebrate the magnate who ordered the work. Instead, the artist begins to put his own signature to it. The names of artists came to be widely known. Painters such as Manuel Panselinos of Thessalonica and Theophanes the Cretan in the sixteenth century and John Hypatos in the seventeenth century are admired figures, to whom many more works than they ever painted are attributed. At the same time, partly owing to the difficulty in building and decorating churches and partly owing to a gradual change in taste, influenced probably by knowledge of the panel pictures that were being painted in the West, an increasing number of individual portable icons were painted, some to hang on the iconostases of churches, but many more for private patrons. It was into these panel icons that the painters put their best work; and amongst these icons there are a few that rank as fine examples of Byzantine art.

Byzantine art thus survived until the eighteenth century. Then the end came. There was now a rich laity in the Christian East that thirsted for culture and longed to patronize the arts. But, even in the circles that surrounded the Patriarchate of Constantinople, the culture that laity sought to imbibe was the culture of the West, the culture that would bring the Greeks into the world of free Christendom and would enable them to look down upon their Oriental Turkish masters. In the provinces the monks and priests mistrusted this occidental trend, with its emphasis on secular philosophies and sciences and its admiration for the hated Franks. In order to keep their faith and traditions pure they closed their doors against the learning that was now dispensed by the authorities at Constantinople. A rigid immutable conservatism, even a deliberate ignorance, reigned in the monasteries that still in the seventeenth century had encouraged Classical learning and individual thought. The artists who followed the old Byzantine tradition were the victims of their times. Their works were despised by the educated laity, while the provincial monks and bishops who still patronized them insisted that they should adhere strictly and without deviation to a fixed tradition. The famous *Painter's Manual* by the Athonite monk Dionysius of Phourna, which cannot have been written before the eighteenth century, is intended for an artistic society where everything has been frozen. It is of great value in describing the traditional methods of technique; but it attempts to lay down strict laws about the theologically correct composition for every holy scene, about the correct pose and costume of the saints and the exact spot which each should occupy. For centuries past Byzantine painters had followed general rules, partly so that the picture should be easily intelligible to the onlooker and partly so that the proper symbolism of colour and gesture should be employed; but they had allowed themselves individual variations and fresh ideas. By the eighteenth century inspiration was stifled and technical advance arrested. Enterprising artists and architects sought new ideas from Italian models; but the bastard results were almost wholly disastrous. Though in recent times there have been brave attempts to recapture the Byzantine style and spirit, no amount of erudition and technical skill can make these efforts more than admirable studies in archaeology.

II

The story of the decline and fall of Byzantine art is of importance because it shows that the style could not survive without the social system and philosophy on which it was based. There was always a popular East Christian art, such as that of the Copts or of the Syrian Christians, which sprang from the same origins as Byzantine art but which never developed far. Only the Armenians, with their geographical and cultural susceptibility to Iranian and further Eastern influences, produced an art capable of growth. Within the heart of the Byzantine Empire there was a lively popular art, seen at its best in the cave-monasteries of Cappadocia. But though it played its part in bringing new conceptions into the art of Constantinople, as did also Armenian art, it could not by itself create a great artistic tradition. Some of the cave-paintings in Cappadocia are of a great and moving beauty. But they are provincial; they are the expressions of an intense but unsophisticated piety. The art of Constantinople is the expression of a complete philosophy.

The basis of the philosophy was constant, but the emphasis sometimes changed. The Byzantines conceived of the Christian commonwealth as the earthly reflection of Heaven, sanctified by the Incarnation. The Christian commonwealth should have been the equivalent of the whole inhabited world, the Oecumene. In fact large tracts of the world were inhabited by infidels, and, as time went on, numbers of Christians seemed to be deserting the true Christian faith. But to the last the Byzantines considered their Empire to be the Oecumene, and used the word in that sense only. Their Emperor and his Court had therefore to represent the Courts of Heaven with their beauty and light; they had to reproduce as best they could the vision given in the Book of Revelations. The Greek Church has always been shy of exact definitions. Its outlook is mystical rather than legalistic. It was only when an accepted, if un-formulated, doctrine was challenged that statements of doctrine were needed. It was only therefore when the system of religious decoration was attacked by the Iconoclasts that the theory of images was evolved. Thenceforward, as a result of a stated theory, there was slightly less fluidity in the development of Byzantine art.

In the earlier centuries that culminated in the splendid age of Justinian the purpose of art was still slightly tinged by pre-Christian notions. The sensual pleasure that Aristotle attributed to art was still recognized, while the Imperial Roman desire to harness art to the glorification of the state had not been entirely Christianized. The Emperor was still depicted in three-dimensional statuary as a glorious figure, almost a god himself. In later centuries he is almost always shown in the act of worshipping or paying some respect to Christ or the Mother of

149. The Church of Rispolozhenia, The Kremlin, Moscow. Fifteenth century onwards

God.[1] Here Justinian's reign is the turning-point. He and the Empress Theodora still had statues made of them in their glory; but their mosaic portraits, such as survive at Ravenna, show them bringing offerings to God. If the Iconoclastic emperors revived the practice of grand Imperial portraits, none have survived the fall of Iconoclasm. But it is unlikely that they did so. They were as conscious as any Iconodule of the divine role of the Emperor, and they disliked any representation of the human form except in a purely lay connection. In architecture too it seems that the full conception of the symbolic meaning of the church-building was slow in developing. The architects of Saint Sophia intended their creation to symbolize the universe. But their aim was to provide within its walls a sense of the infinite space of heaven, not to make every portion correspond with a definite part of heaven or episode in the heavenly story. Saint Sophia certainly stands apart. It was to the last the great ceremonial church of the Empire. Along with the Sacred Palace it represented the Court of Heaven; they were the setting in which the Emperor moved as the vice-regent of God. To the last, though the ceremonies became fewer and less splendid, the great church was used as much for the glory of the Empire as for the celebration of the Liturgy. For their more intimate devotions the Byzantines began to prefer smaller shrines, where they could feel more closely connected with Christ and his Mother and the saints whom they loved.

The construction of Saint Sophia belonged to an age when the Roman idea of Empire was still dominant, when Majesty expressed itself in size and magnificence. The political troubles of the seventh century, followed by the Iconoclastic controversy in which the whole theory of the outward expression of the idea of the Christian commonwealth was debated and decided, pruned away something of the worldly splendour and left an art more perfectly attuned, perhaps, than any art before or since with the ideas and concepts of the Empire of God on earth. It was an aristocratic art. Its great figure mosaics are somewhat distant and of another world, though their eyes pierce into the human soul. It is still magnificent, but the glitter is transformed into luminosity, and is balanced and restrained. It is the art of an Imperial city assured of its spiritual

1. Where Imperial figures appear alone, such as the Empress Zoe on the crown of Monomachus or the Empress Irene on the Pala d'Oro, they are part of an all-over design. The same is probably true of the now isolated panel of the Emperor Alexander in the north gallery of Saint Sophia.

and physical greatness. To the peasants of the countryside it was rather too remote. They preferred a homelier, more anecdotal art, with a stronger emphasis on the human aspect of the Gospel story, told, often, with severity and harshness, but with an appeal to the human emotions rather than to an Idea.

The disasters of the late eleventh century and the problems that followed destroyed the complacency of Byzantium. The Idea was besmirched; and the humanity of the provinces penetrated into the Capital. The superb technique of the Constantinopolitan artists raised the new art to be an Imperial art. But it was less perfect than the art of the high Byzantine period, and less intellectualized. It allowed for human emotions, reaching out even into a certain poignant fantasy. There was need for a return to Classical studies to achieve the new humanized synthesis which reached its highest expression in the art of the early fourteenth century, of which the Church of Our Saviour in Chora is the great surviving example. How it might have developed had the Empire survived we cannot tell and it is idle to conjecture. It may be that the determination of the Byzantines in those latter days to keep their religion pure and to cling to their own traditions would have resulted in much the same sort of stagnation as befell their art when they lost their political freedom; for it was above all the highly educated government at Constantinople that guaranteed a constant renewal of cultural activity and fashion.

Little of Byzantine secular art has survived. The loss is to be regretted; but Byzantine art was essentially a religious art. Byzantine theory dismissed as inadequate the Aristotelian notion that the object of art was to please the senses. It was essentially based on the concept of the image as being the shadow of the original. The image could not exist without an original. It was therefore part of the original with something of the qualities of the original. The simple worshipper in his painted church was surrounded not just by paint but by presences. The pictures that he saw were part of the persons and scenes that they depicted. The sophisticated courtier whose eye wandered round the glowing sequence of mosaics in the Palace chapels found himself in mystical contact with Christ and the saints whose glances were fixed so searchingly upon him. That was the function of art, to increase the understanding of the divine beyond the finite limits of the human mind.

All the arts are pleasing to the Lord, who created our senses, whether it be music, the nearest to the visual arts with it mathematical foundation, or the more sensual arts. Marble smooth to the touch, the sweet scent of incense, even the delicate flavour of wine, could all play their part in the worship of the Creator. Secular art, too, was not excluded; for to create beauty wherever it might be was to help in the divine order. But sight was the first of the senses, just as light was the first of the elements; and light meant colour and the form that colour made and distinguished. Even sculpture was considered as a supplement to the pictorial arts, in providing an additional element of light and shade. Architecture was a practical, functional art; and even the Lord must have his temples and the Emperor his halls. But though a church was primarily necessary to provide an enclosed and sheltered place for the celebration of worship, the holiest duty of the architect was to provide a proper setting in which the luminous images of the Hosts of Heaven could join the faithful on earth in the Liturgy.

Had Iconoclasm triumphed, Byzantine art, for all its brilliant beginning, would doubtless have followed the line that Islamic art was to take. It would have become an art of pattern, a purely decorative art, quite unable to express the faith that was the finest and most creative element in Byzantine culture. The triumph of the Iconodules was the triumph of the true Byzantium. It gave to the Byzantines a formulated purpose for their art. And it was no mean purpose. It aimed to interpret the doctrine of the Incarnation in terms of visible beauty and of light.

Catalogue of Illustrations

14. CHURCH OF S. COSTANZA, *Rome*. Late fourth century. General view. (Photo: Alinari.)

Lit: H. Steen, 'Les Mosaiques de l'église de Sainte Constance à Rome', *Dumbarton Oaks Papers*, 12, 1958, pp. 59 ff; G. Matthiae, *Mosaici Mediovali delle chiese di Roma*, 1967, pp. 3 ff; W. Oakeshott, *The Mosaics of Rome*, 1967, pp. 61-5, pls. I, VII, 34-41.

15. CHURCH OF S. MARIA MAGGIORE, *Rome*. General view of interior. (Photo: Alinari.) The church was built by Pope Sixtus III between 432 and 440. The iconography partly illustrates the decisions of the Council of Ephesus.

Lit: C. Cecchelli, *I mosaici della basilica di S. Maria Maggiore*, 1956; A. Grabar, *Byzantium from the Death of Theodosius to the Rise of Islam*, pp. 145-8.

16. THE PRESENTATION. Mosaic in the nave of *S. Maria Maggiore*. (Photo: Alinari.)

17. SAINTS ONESIPHORUS AND PORPHYRIUS. Mosaics in the dome of *Saint George, Thessalonica*. Late fourth century. (Photo: Hirmer.) The building almost certainly formed part of the palace of Theodosius I at Thessalonica, and may not have been transformed into a church until about 400.

Lit: H. Torp, *Mosaikkene i St Georgrotunden*, 1956; R. F. Hoddinott, *Early Byzantine Churches in Macedonia and Southern Serbia*, pp. 108-23; A. Grabar, 'A propos les mosaiques de la coupole de Saint-Georges à Salonique', *Cahiers Archéologiques*, XVII, 1967, pp. 59 ff.

18. MAUSOLEUM OF GALLA PLACIDIA, *Ravenna. c. 425*. General view of interior. (Photo: Alinari.)

Lit: G. Bovini, *Il cosidetto Mausoleo di Galla Placidia in Ravenna*, 1950; R. Krautheimer, *Early Christian and Byzantine Architecture*, 1965, pp. 137-8; J. Beckwith, *Early Christian and Byzantine Art*, p. 15.

19. MAUSOLEUM OF GALLA PLACIDIA. Mosaics in central vault. (Photo: German Archaelogical Institute, Rome.)

20. WOODEN DOOR. 422-40. *Rome, S. Sabina*. (Photo: Alinari.)

Lit: A. Grabar, *Christian Iconography*, pp. 142-5.

21. THE ASCENSION OF ELIJAH. Panel of 20 above.

22. A PHILOSOPHER BETWEEN JONAH AND ORANT AND THE GOOD SHEPHERD. Carving on a sarcophagus in *S. Maria Antica, Rome*. Probably late third century. (Photo: Hirmer.) The philosopher represents the deceased.

Lit: M. Gough, op. cit., p. 90, pls. 14, 15.

23. THE GOOD SHEPHERD BETWEEN TWO RAMS. Carving on a sarcophagus in the *Museo Lateranense, Rome*. Fourth century. (Photo: Anderson.)

Lit: J. Wilpert, *Sarcofagi Cristiani Antichi*, 1929, I, p. 7, pls. 1-2; W. F. Volbach, *Frühchristliche Kunst*, 1958, p. 9, pl. 6.

24. GOLD COIN OF THE EMPEROR GALLIENUS. *Milan, Museo Civico*. (Photo: Museum.)

Lit: G. Mathew, *Byzantine Aesthetics*, pp. 14-15.

25. THEODOSIUS I AND HIS SONS RECEIVING GIFTS FROM THE BARBARIANS. Detail from the base for the Egyptian obelisk in the Hippodrome (at Meidan), *Constantinople. c. 390*. (Photo: Hirmer.)

Lit: A. Grabar, *Sculpture Byzantine de Constantinople*, 1963, pp. 25 ff; idem, *Byzantium from the Death of Theodosius*, pp. 219-20.

26. THEODOSIUS I AND HIS SONS, WITH ALLEGORICAL FIGURES. Silver missorium. Dated 488. *Madrid, Academia de la Historia*. (Photo: Giraudon.)

Lit: R. Delbrueck, op. cit., p. 67; W. F. Volbach, *Frühchristliche Kunst*, 1958, pp. 55-6; J. Beckwith, *The Art of Constantinople*, 1963, pp. 15-16; A. Grabar, *Byzantium from the Death of Theodosius*, p. 303, pls. 348-51.

3. Details from the Missorium of Theodosius, 26 above. (Photos: Mas.)

29. MOUNTED EMPEROR. Ivory known as the Barberini Ivory. *Paris, Musée du Louvre.* The Emperor has been identified as Zeno or Anastasius, but is now generally considered to be Justinian I and is to be dated *c.* 530. (Photo: Hirmer.) Lit: R. Delbrueck, *Die Consulardiptychen,* 1929, No. 48; A. Grabar, *L'Empereur dans l'art byzantin,* 1936, pp. 48–9; W. F. Volbach, *Elfenarbeiten der spätantike und des frühen Mittelaltes,* 1952, No. 48; idem, *Frühchristliche Kunst,* p. 87; J. Beckwith, op. cit., pp. 38–40, pl. 49.

30. THE EMPRESS THEODORA AND HER COURT. Mosaic panel in *S. Vitale, Ravenna. c.* 547. (Photo: Alinari.) Lit: See 46 below.

31. OLD AND NEW TESTAMENT SCENES. On an ivory reliquary casket. *c.* 370. *Brescia, Museo Cristiano.* (Photo: Hirmer.) Lit: W. F. Volbach, *Elfenbeinarbeiten,* No. 107; A. Grabar, *Christian Iconography,* pp. 137–8, pls. 333–7.

32. BRIDAL CASKET OF SECUNDUS AND PROJECTA. Silver. Late fourth century. *London, British Museum.* Found on the Esquiline Hill. The decoration shows a mixture of pagan and Christian imagery. (Photo: Hirmer.) Lit: E. Kitzinger, *Early Medieval Art in the British Museum,* 1940, pp. 19–20, pl. 10; A. Grabar, *Byzantium from the Death of Theodosius,* pp. 286, 298, pls. 344–5.

33. CHURCH OF SAINT SYMEON (QALAT SIMAN), in *Northern Syria.* Late fifth century. (Photo: Derek Hill.) This huge martyrium, built in honour of Saint Symeon the Stylite, was unique but served as a model for many smaller churches in the Antiochene Patriarchate. Lit: H. C. Butler, *Early Churches in Syria,* 1929, pp. 97 ff; J. Lassus, *Sanctuaires chrétiens de Syrie,* 1947, p. 135; R. Krautheimer, *Early Christian and Byzantine Architecture,* 1965, pp. 111–13.

34. CHURCH OF SAINT SYMEON. See 33 above.

35. PRINCESS JULIANA ANICIA. Illustration from Ms. of Dioscurides' *Materia Medica,* made in Constantinople in 512. *Vienna, Oesterreichische Nationalbibliothek.* (Photo: Bildarchiv.) Juliana Anicia, who was the daughter of the Emperor Olybrius and the granddaughter of Valentinian III and died in 527, was the last great private patron of the arts in Byzantium for about five centuries. She is shown here seated between Magnanimity and Prudence. Lit: E. Diez, 'Die Miniaturen des Wiennes Dioscurides', *Byzantinische Denkmaler,* III, 1903, pp. 1 ff; A. von Premerstein, K. Wessely, J. Mantuani, *Dioscurides, Codex Aniciae Julianae, phototypice editus,* 1906; A. Grabar, *Byzantium from the Death of Theodosius,* p. 197, pls. 214–15; J. Beckwith, *Early Christian and Byzantine Art,* p. 57, pl. 105.

36–43. SAINT SOPHIA (Aya Sofya), *Constantinople.* Built 532–7. Architects: Anthemius of Tralles and Isidore of Miletus. The first dome collapsed in 558 and a new steeper dome was completed, by the younger Isidore of Miletus, in 563. This dome had to be repaired after an earthquake in 989 by the Armenian architect, Tirdat. More repairs to the dome and the apse were needed after an earthquake in 1346. The external buttresses were added at various times from the later sixth century onwards. The minarets and present outbuildings are of Ottoman construction. (Photos: Josephine Powell, Hirmer, Phototech Marburg.) Lit: It is only possible to make selections from the vast bibliography on the building. E. H. Swift, *Hagia Sophia,* 1940, remains the standard book in English, though it will be superseded by a complete structural study by R. Van Nice, to be published shortly. There is an authoritative summary in R. Krautheimer, op. cit., pp. 153–70 and notes, pp. 336–8.

44. CHURCH OF SAINT IRENE, *Constantinople*. General view. (Photo: Josephine Powell.) The church was built in the years following 532, but was extensively remodelled after a fire in 564 and again to a lesser extent after an earthquake in about 740, and by the Turks in 1453. The original domed basilica has been modified by these alterations.
Lit: W. S. George, *The Church of Saint Eirene*, 1913; A. van Millingen, *Byzantine Churches in Constantinople*, 1912, pp. 84 ff; J. Ebersolt and A. Thiers, *Les Eglises de Constantinople*, 1913, pp. 57 ff; R. Janin, *La Géographie ecclésiastique de l'Empire byzantin*, 1ère. partie, *Le Siège de Constantinople*, III, *Les églises et les monastères*, 1953, pp. 108 ff; R. Krautheimer, op. cit., pp. 180–81.

45A, B. CHURCHES OF SAINT JOHN *at Ephesus and* SAINTS SERGIUS AND BACCHUS *at Constantinople*. Ground plans. The church of Saint John, of which little now remains, seems to have been very similar in design to the church of the Holy Apostles in Constantinople, which was pulled down soon after 1453, but which had been copied by the architects of Saint Mark's in Venice. The Church of Saints Sergius and Bacchus is akin to the church of S. Vitale at Ravenna. The cruciform domed basilica, as represented by Saint John, and the octagonal centralized double-shell, as represented by Saints Sergius and Bacchus, are the two extreme styles of Justinian's time. The plan of Saint Sophia lies somewhere in between.
Lit: R. Krautheimer, op. cit., pp. 161–3, 169–70, 175–7.

46. CHURCH OF S. VITALE, *Ravenna*. Built 538–45. General view of interior. The mosaics date from 546–8. (Photo: Hirmer.)
Lit: G. Erola, *Felix Ravenna*, X, 1913, pp. 427 ff, XI, 1913, pp. 459 ff, XXI, 1916, pp. 879 ff; R. Bartocini, ibid., XXXVIII, 1931, pp. 77 ff, and XLI, 1932, pp. 133 ff; F. W. Deichmann, ibid., LX, 1952, pp. 5 ff.

47. S. VITALE. South wall of apse. The mosaic in the lunette shows the sacrifices of Abel and Melchisedech. (Photo: Hirmer.)

48. CHURCH OF S. APOLLINARE IN CLASSE, near *Ravenna*. Consecrated in 549. View of apse. (Photo: Alinari.)
Lit: M. Mazzotti, *La basilica di Santa Apollinare in Classe*, 1954; R. Krautheimer, op. cit., pp. 195–6.

49. Dedicatory INSCRIPTION in *Saints Sergius and Bacchus, Constantinople*. On a frieze running round the church, in honour of Justinian and Theodora. (Photo: Josephine Powell.)
Lit: A. van Millingen, op. cit., pp. 73–4; J. Ebersolt and A. Thiers, op. cit., p. 20.

50. THE TRANSFIGURATION. Mosaic in apse of monastery church of *Saint Catherine, Mount Sinai*. *c*. 540. (Photo: by courtesy of the Alexandria, Michigan, Princeton Archaeological Expedition to Mount Sinai.)
Lit: G. H. Forsyth, 'The monastery of St. Catherine at Mount Sinai', *Dumbarton Oaks Papers*, 22, 1968, pp. 1–20.

51. SAINT MARK. Miniature from the Codex Rossanensis. Probably Constantinopolitan work. Mid sixth century. *Rossano, Museo Diocesano*. (Photo: Giraudon.)
Lit: A. Munoz, *Il Codice purpureo di Rossano ed il frammento Sinopense*, 1907; A. Grabar, *Byzantium from the Death of Theodosius*, pp. 204–8; J. Beckwith, *Early Christian and Byzantine Art*, pp. 58–9.

52. THE LAST SUPPER and other scenes. From the Codex Rossanensis. (Photo: Giraudon.)

53. REBEKAH AT THE WELL. Miniature from the Vienna Genesis. Mid sixth century. *Vienna, Nationalbibliothek*. (Photo: Library.) An Eastern origin, such as Antioch or Jerusalem, has been suggested by the codex; but it is more likely

that all the codices written on purple parchment came from the Imperial workshops at Constantinople.
Lit: H. Gerstinger, *Die Wiener Genesis*, 1931; E. Wellesz, *The Vienna Genesis*, 1960; G. Mathew, op. cit,, pp. 82-4; J. Beckwith, op. cit., pp. 58-9.
54. THE ARCHANGEL MICHAEL. Panel of ivory diptych. Early sixth century. *London, The British Museum.* (Photo: Hirmer.)
Lit: W. F. Volbach, *Elfenbeinarbeiten*, No. 109; J. Beckwith, op. cit., p. 37.
55. A POET. Detail from ivory diptych. Mid sixth century. *Monza, Cathedral treasury.* (Photo: Hirmer.)
Lit: R. Delbrueck, op. cit., No. 437 W. F. Volbach, op. cit., No. 107.
56. THE COMMUNION OF THE APOSTLES. On a paten found at Stuma in Syria. Silver and silver-gilt, with control stamp of Justin II (565-78). *Istanbul, Archaeological Museum.* (Photo: Hirmer.)
Lit: W. F. Volbach, *Frühchristliche Kunst*, p. 91; J. Beckwith, *Art of Constantinople*, 1961, pp. 46-7.
57. CHAIR OF ARCHBISHOP MAXIMIAN. Ivory. *c.* 548. *Ravenna, Archbishop's Palace.* (Photo: Anderson.)
Lit: W. F. Volbach, op. cit., No. 140; J. Beckwith, op. cit., pp. 52-3.
58. CAMEL. Detail from floor-mosaics. *Great Palace, Constantinople.* (Photo: Josephine Powell.) The date of these mosaics has been much disputed. Archaeological evidence indicates that they were made after the reconstruction of the Palace by Marcian in about 455; and some scholars date them as late as the reign of Justin II or even of Tiberius. But pictorial floor-mosaics seem to have been given up long before that date, perhaps because of a growing dislike for treading upon the representation of man, who is made in God's image. It seems more natural to assign them, as do the excavators, to the later fifth or, at latest, the early sixth century, 'for stylistic, iconographic and topographical reasons' (A. Grabar, see below).
Lit: *The Great Palace of the Byzantine Emperors, First Report*, 1947, *Second Report*, 1958, esp. pp. 161 ff; review by C. Mango and I. Lavin in *Art Bulletin*, XLII, 1960, preferring a later date, Mango suggesting the reign of Tiberius; J. Beckwith, *Art of Constantinople*, pp. 29-31, suggesting the reign of Justin II; A. Grabar, *Byzantium from the Death of Theodosius*, pp. 102-5.
59. MONUMENTAL HEAD. Detail from floor-mosaics. *Great Palace, Constantinople.* (Photo: Josephine Powell.)
60. PHILANTHROPIA. Detail from the Consular diptych of Clementinus. Ivory. 513. *Liverpool, City Museum.* (Photo: Hirmer.)
Lit: R. Delbrueck, *Consulardiptychen*, No. 16; W. F. Volbach, *Elfenbeinarbeiten*, No. 15.
61. SAINT DEMETRIUS AND DONOR. Mosaic panel. *Church of Saint Demetrius, Thessalonica.* Mid seventh century. (Photo: Hirmer.)
Lit: C. Diehl, M. Le Tourneau and H. Saladin, *Les Monuments chrétiens de Salonique, Monuments de l'art byzantin*, IV, pp. 61 ff; G. and M. Soteriou, *The Basilica of Saint Demetrios at Thessaloniki* (in Greek), 1952; E. Kitzinger, 'Byzantine Art in the period between Justinian and Iconoclasm', *XIth International Congress of Byzantine Studies*, 1958, pp. 23 ff; R. F. Hoddinott, *Early Byzantine Churches*, pp. 125 ff; R. Krautheimer, op. cit., pp. 95-7.
62. GOLD SOLIDUS OF JUSTINIAN II. Mint of Constantinople. *c.* 690. Bust of Christ on obverse, Emperor on reverse. *Dumbarton Oaks Collection.*
63. PROCESSION OF ICONS. From the Lorsch Gospels. Executed for the Emperor Charles the Great, *c.* 800, probably at Aachen. *Alba Julia, Batthanyaeum.* (Photo: Robert Braunmüller.) This is a Western manuscript, but it illustrates a typical

procession of icons or relics, such as had become a regular occurrence in the Eastern and Western Churches by the beginning of the eighth century.

Lit: W. Braunfels, *The Lorsch Gospels*, 1967; J. Beckwith, *Early Christian and Byzantine Art*, p. 37.

64A, B, C THE EMPEROR PROSTRATE BEFORE CHRIST. Mosaic panel over the Imperial Door from the narthex into the church in *Saint Sophia, Constantinople*. *c*. 890. (Photos: Byzantine Institute Inc.) The Emperor, who is almost certainly Leo VI, is shown in the act of *proskynesis*.

Lit: *The Mosaics of Haghia Sophia, Istanbul, First Preliminary Report: The Mosaics of the Narthex*, 1933; A. Grabar, *L'Iconoclasme byzantin*, 1953, pp. 234 ff; C. Mango, *The Mosaics of St Sophia at Istanbul (Dumbarton Oaks Studies VIII)*, 1962, pp. 27 ff.

65. CROSS IN MOSAIC in the apse of *Saint Irene, Constantinople*. *c*. 750. (Photo: Josephine Powell.) The Cross was probably put up when the building was reconditioned after an earthquake. In its stark simplicity it is probably typical of Iconoclastic church decoration.

Lit: See 44 above.

66. SILVER COIN OF THEOPHILUS. Constantinople. *c*. 830. Cross on three steps on obverse, Emperor's inscription on reverse. *Washington, D.C., Dumbarton Oaks Collection*. (Photo: Byzantine Institute Inc.)

67. CHARIOTEER. Silk compound from the tomb of Charlemagne at Aachen. Late eighth century. *Aachen, Cathedral Treasury*. (Photo: Ann Münchow.)

Lit: *Masterpieces of Byzantine Art, Edinburgh–London*, 1958, No. 56; J. Beckwith, *The Art of Constantinople*, pp. 58-9.

68. BRONZE DOORS, leading from the narthex into the church of *Saint Sophia, Constantinople*. Original date uncertain, repaired by Theophilus in 841. (Photo: Marburg Bildarchiv.)

Lit: W. R. Lethaby and H. Swainson, *The Church of Sancta Sophia, Constantinople*, 1894, pp. 267 ff.

69. SILVER BUCKET with mythological scenes, with control of stamp of Heraclius I (613–29). *Vienna, Kunsthistorisches Museum*. (Photo: Hirmer.)

Lit: L. Mazulewitsch, *Byzantinische Antike*, 1929, pp. 37 ff; J. Beckwith, *Art of Constantinople*, pp. 49–51.

70. SILENUS. From a silver dish with the control stamp of Heraclius I (613–29). *Leningrad, Hermitage Museum*. (Photo: Hirmer.)

Lit: Mazulewitsch, op. cit., pp. 18 ff; D. Talbot Rice, *The Art of Byzantium*, 1959, p. 306, pl. 75; A. Banck, *Byzantine Art in the Collections in the USSR* (in Russian and English), 1965, Nos. 88-9.

71. THE PATRIARCH NICEPHORUS VICTORIOUS OVER THE ICONOCLAST JOHN THE GRAMMARIAN. Miniature from the Chludov Psalter. Late ninth century. *Moscow, State Historical Museum*. Probably copied from a monastic manuscript nearer in date to the Council of 815, when Iconoclasm was temporarily re-introduced. The upper drawing shows Saint Peter crushing Simon Magus.

Lit: J. Ebersolt, *La Miniature Byzantine*, 1926, pp. 17-19; C. Diehl, *La Peinture Byzantine*, 1938, p. 43, pl. LXXII; J. Beckwith, *Early Christian and Byzantine Art*, pp. 83-4, pl. 149.

72. MONASTERY CHURCHES OF HOSIOS LUKAS IN PHOCIS. Ground plan. The Catholicon is a good example of the Greek-cross-octagon design, the Church of the Theotokos to the north a good example of the cross-in-square, or quincunx, design. The former dates from *c*. 1020, the latter from some twenty years later. The latter is not absolutely rectangular, being slightly tilted to the north, to suit the site.

Lit: R. W. Schultz and S. H. Barnsley, *The Monastery of Saint Luke of Styris*, 1901; R. Krautheimer, op. cit., pp. 243-4, 275-8.

73. CHRIST PANTOCRATOR. Mosaic in the dome of the church at *Daphni, Attica*. (Photo: Josephine Powell.) For the dating, see 99 below.

74. ARCHANGEL GABRIEL. Mosaic on the north wall of the apse of the church at *Daphni*. (Photo: Josephine Powell.) See 99 below.

75. THE MOTHER OF GOD. Mosaic in the apse of *Saint Sophia, Constantinople*. (Photo: by courtesy of Dumbarton Oaks Field Committee.) From its style the mosaic has sometimes been thought to date after 1346, when an earthquake severely damaged the east end of the church. But a careful examination of the mosaic and its setting seems to prove that it dates from the late ninth century and was almost certainly the representation of the Mother of God to which the Patriarch Photius refers in the sermon delivered in Saint Sophia on 29 March 867.
Lit: A. Grabar, *L'Iconoclasme byzantin*, pp. 189 ff; C. Mango, *The Mosaics of St Sophia at Istanbul*, pp. 80 ff; C. Mango and E. J. Hawkins, 'The Apse Mosaics of St Sophia at Istanbul. Report on work carried out in 1964', *Dumbarton Oaks Papers*, XI, 1965, giving the technical details and a full discussion.

76. THE MOTHER OF GOD 'HODEGETRIA'. Ivory statuette. Twelfth century. *Victoria and Albert Museum, London*. (Photo: Museum.)
Lit: J. Beckwith, ' "Mother of God showing the way", a Byzantine Ivory Statuette of the Theotokos Hodegetria', *The Connoisseur*, CL, 1962, pp. 2 ff.

77. MOSES RECEIVING THE LAW. Miniature from Psalter. *Paris, Bibliothèque Nationale*, Gr. 139. Mid tenth century. (Photo: Hirmer.)
Lit: K. Weitzmann, *Byzantinische Buchmalerei des IX und X Jahrhunderts*, 1935, pp. 8-13, and *Greek Mythology in Byzantine Art*, 1951, pp. 206-8; H. Buchthal, *The Paris Psalter*, 1938; Bibliothèque Nationale, *Byzance et la France Médiévale*, 1958, No. 10.

78. SAINT MATTHEW AT HIS DESK. Miniature from Gospel. *Rome, Vatican Library*, Cod. Chis. VIII, 54. Twelfth century. (Photo: Vatican.)

79. DONOR WITH THE MOTHER OF GOD. Frontispiece to Gospel in *National Gallery of Victoria, Melbourne*, formerly in the Dyson Perrins Collection. *c.* 1100. (Photo: Museum.) The manuscript is unique in that the writer, illuminator and donor were the same one man and that we know his name, the monk Theophanes.
Lit: H. Buchthal, *An Illuminated Byzantine Gospel Book of about 1100 A.D.*, Special Bulletin of the National Gallery of Victoria, 1961.

80. THE EMPEROR ALEXANDER. Mosaic in the north gallery of *Saint Sophia, Constantinople*. 912-13. Alexander reigned as senior Emperor for only one year, and the mosaic can positively be dated from that period. (Photo: Byzantine Institute Inc.)
Lit: P. Underwood and E. J. Hawkins, 'The Mosaics of Haghia Sophia at Istanbul. A Report on Work done in 1959 and 1960. The Portrait of the Emperor Alexander', *Dumbarton Oaks Papers*, 1961, pp. 189-217; J. Beckwith, *Early Christian and Byzantine Art*, pp. 89-90.

81. THE MOTHER OF GOD. Mosaic over the door leading from the south vestibule into the narthex at *Saint Sophia, Constantinople*. To be dated probably about 1000. The Virgin sits between the Emperors Constantine, the founder of the city, and Justinian, the builder of Saint Sophia. (Photo: Marburg Bildarchiv.)
Lit: *The Mosaics of Haghia Sophia, Istanbul, Secondary Preliminary Report: The Mosaics of the South Vestibule*, 1936; V. N. Lazarev, *History of Byzantine Painting* (in Russian), 1948, I, pp. 88 ff; D. Talbot Rice, *The Art of Byzantium*, pp. 56, 319, pl. 129; J. Beckwith, *The Art of Constantinople*, pp. 97-8.

82. GOLD AND ENAMEL ARMBAND. Ninth century. *Thessalonica, Archaeological Museum.* (Photo: Hirmer.)
   Lit: K. Wessel, *Byzantine Enamels*, 1969, No. 14.

83. GOLD FILIGREE EARRINGS. *Athens, Benaki Museum.* Usually dated seventh century, but similar designs appear on tenth- and eleventh-century work, such as a pendant in the Athens Archaelogical Museum, Helen Stathatos Collection. (Photo: Hirmer.)
   Lit: B. Segall, *Katalog der Goldschmiede-Arbeiten, Museum Benaki*, 1938, No. 246; *Byzantine Art, an European Art, Athens, Catalogue*, No. 420.

84. ONYX PATEN with enamel medallion set in the centre, depicting the Last Supper. *Venice, Treasury of Saint Mark. c. 900.* (Photo: Giraudon.)
   Lit: K. Wessel, *Byzantine Enamels*, No. 15.

85. RELIQUARY in enamel for fragments of the True Cross, *Limburg, a.d. Lahn, Cathedral Treasury.* Mid tenth century. Reverse of panel. (Photo: Hirmer.) The space for the relic is on the obverse, which is also decorated in enamel. The panel is framed in gold, with inscriptions on each side, and fits into a gold case with a sliding lid. The inscription on the obverse names the Emperors Constantine and Romanus as having decorated the reliquary and that on the reverse names Basil the Proedros as having made the case. Basil, who was the bastard son of Romanus I, was a prominent minister from 944 to 985, and was given the title of Proedros in 963.
   Lit: D. Talbot Rice, *Art of Byzantium*, p. 318, pls. 124-6; J. Beckwith, *The Art of Constantinople*, pp. 87-92; A. Frolow, *La Relique de la Vraie Croix*, 1961, pp. 233-7; K. Wessel, *Byzantine Enamels*, No. 22.

86. SHROUD OF SAINT GERMAIN. Silk. *Auxerre, Church of Saint-Eusèbe.* Tenth century. Presumably woven in the Imperial workshops. (Photo: Giraudon.)
   Lit: D. Talbot Rice, *Art of Byzantium*, p. 320, pl. 132; J. Beckwith, *Early Christian and Byzantine Art*, p. 99, pl. 186.

87. ONYX CHALICE. Set in silver gilt, with jewels round rim and base. *Venice, Treasury of Saint Mark. c. 1000.* (Photo: Alinari.)
   Lit: A. Pasini, *Il Tesoro di San Marco*, 1886.

88. CONSTANTINE VII CROWNED BY CHRIST. Ivory panel. 945. *Moscow, Municipal Museum of Fine Art.* (Photo: Hirmer.) As Constantine was first crowned when he was a small child, this must celebrate his taking over supreme power at the end of 944.
   Lit: A. Goldschmidt and K. Weitzmann, *Die Byzantinischen Elfenbeinskulpturen des X bis XIII Jahrhunderts*, 1934, No. 35; A. Banck, *Byzantine Art in the Collections in the USSR*, Nos. 124-5; J. Beckwith, *Early Christian and Byzantine Art*, p. 99, pl. 173.

89. KING DAVID. Miniature from Psalter. *Paris, Bibliothèque Nationale*, Gr. 139. Mid tenth century. (Photo: Hirmer.)
   Lit: See 77 above.

90. SAINT DEMETRIUS. Enamel medallion. *Paris, Musée de Cluny.* Mid eleventh century. (Photo: Hirmer.) The medallion, with nine others, comes from the frame of an icon in the Georgian monastery of Djumati, but is undoubtedly from the Imperial workshops.
   Lit: N. Kondakov, *Histoire et Monuments des Emaux byzantine*, 1892, pp. 280-85; C. Amiranachvili, *Les Emaux de Géorgie*, 1961, p. 20; *Byzantine Art, an European Art*, No. 468; K. Wessel, *Byzantine Enamels*, No. 40.

91. DETAIL OF IVORY CASKET, known as the Veroli Casket. *London, Victoria and Albert Museum.* Tenth or eleventh century. (Photo: Hirmer.)

92. MYTHOLOGICAL FIGURES. On enamelled glass bowl. *Venice, Treasury of Saint Mark's*. Eleventh century. (Photo: Böhm.)
Lit: K. Weitzmann, *Greek Mythology in Byzantine Art*, p. 203; J. Beckwith, *Early Christian and Byzantine Art*, p. 107, pl. 196.

93. CAVE CHURCH. Tokali Kilise, near Göreme, *Cappadocia*. Ninth-tenth centuries. View of interior. (Photo: Josephine Powell.)
Lit: M. Restle, *Byzantine Painting in Asia Minor*, 1967, I, pp. 23-7, 35-41, II, pls. 61 ff.

94. DANCERS AND HORSES. Miniature from the *Cynegetica* of Oppian. *Venice, Biblioteca Marciana*, Gr. 479. Early eleventh century. (Photo: Böhm.)
Lit: K. Weitzmann, *Greek Mythology in Byzantine Art*, pp. 93 ff, fully illustrated.

95A, B. DANCERS. Enamel plaques from a crown sent by the Emperor Constantine IX to Hungary. *Budapest, National Museum. c.* 1050. (Photo: Museum.) The diadem was probably intended for the Hungarian queen, Anastasia of Russia, wife of Andrew I.
Lit: M. von Barany-Oberschall, *The Crown of the Emperor Constantine Monomachos*, 1937; K. Wessel, *Byzantine Enamels*, No. 32.

96. THE EMPRESS IRENE DUCAENA. Enamel plaque from the Pala d'Oro in *Saint Mark's, Venice. c.* 1100. (Photo: Böhm.) The enamel plaques set into the Pala are of various dates and varying quality.
Lit: O. Demus, *The Church of San Marco in Venice*, 1960, pp. 23 ff; G. Lorenzoni, *La Pala d'Oro di San Marco*, 1965; K. Wessel, *Byzantine Enamels*, No. 46.

97. HOLY LUKE THE STYRIOTE. Mosaic in the north transept of the Katholikon of *Hosios Lukas in Phocis. c.* 1020. (Photo: Josephine Powell.)
Lit: C. Diehl, *L'Eglise et les mosaiques du Convent de Saint Luc en Phocide*, 1889; R. W. Schultz and S. H. Barnsley, *The Monastery of Saint Luke of Styris*, 1901; E. Diez and O. Demus, *Byzantine Mosaics in Greece, Hosios Lucas and Daphne*, 1931; (for the architecture) R. Krautheimer, *Early Christian and Byzantine Architecture*, pp. 275 ff.

98. THE ANASTASIS. Part of a mosaic panel in the catholikon of the *Nea Moni, on Chios*. Mid eleventh century. (Photo: P. Papachatzidakis.)
Lit: O. Wulff, 'Die Mosaiken der Nea Moni von Chios', *Byzantinische Zeitschrift*, XXV, 1925, pp. 115 ff; N. V. Lazarev, *History of Byzantine Painting*, I, pp. 91 ff; J. Beckwith, *Early Christian and Byzantine Art*, pp. 109-10.

99. BIRTH OF THE MOTHER OF GOD. Mosaic panel in the north transept of the church at *Daphni. c.* 1075. (Photo: Josephine Powell.) Many authorities date the mosaics *c.* 1100, but Diez and Demus give literary reasons for dating them before 1080; and the political state of the Empire would have made it impossible to carry out an expensive work of art in the Greek province between 1080 and 1115.
Lit: E. Diez and O. Demus, *Byzantine Mosaics in Greece*, esp. pp. 92 ff; M. Chadzidakis, *Byzantine Monuments in Attica and Boeotia*, 1956, pp. 17 ff; J. Beckwith, *Early Christian and Byzantine Art*, pp. 120-21.

100. THE EMPEROR NICEPHORUS BOTANIATES AND THE EMPRESS MARIA THE ALANIAN. Miniature from the Homilies of Saint John Chrysostom. *Paris, Bibliothèque Nationale*, Coislin Gr. 79. *c.* 1078. (Photo: Hirmer.) The Emperor's portrait is lifelike, the Empress's more conventional. Anna Comnena, who knew her well, describes her far more vividly in the *Alexiad*, bk. III, ch. 2.
Lit: *Byzance et la France Médiévale*, No. 29; J. Beckwith, *Art of Constantinople*, pp. 116-17.

101. CHRIST ENTHRONED BETWEEN THE EMPEROR CONSTANTINE IX AND THE EMPRESS ZOE. Mosaic panel in the south gallery of *Saint Sophia, Constantinople*

(Photo: Byzantine Institute Inc.) It was probably first put up in 1028, portraying Zoe's first husband, Romanus III, instead of Constantine. At some time the heads, including Christ's, were defaced, perhaps by Michael V when he exiled Zoe in 1042, and were replaced after her restoration later that year and her marriage to Constantine.

Lit: *The Mosaics of Haghia Sophia at Istanbul, Third Preliminary Report, The Imperial Portraits of the South Gallery*, 1942; D. Talbot Rice, *Art of Byzantium*, p. 320, pls. XIII, 133; J. Beckwith, *Art of Constantinople*, pp. 104-5.

102A, B THE MOTHER OF GOD BETWEEN THE EMPEROR JOHN II COMNENUS AND THE EMPRESS IRENE THE HUNGARIAN. Mosaic panel in the south gallery of *Saint Sophia, Constantinople. c.* 1118. (Photos: Byzantine Institute Inc.) A portrait of their son Alexius, apparently by another hand, was added in a side panel, probably in 1122, when he was crowned co-Emperor.

Lit: *The Mosaics of Haghia Sophia at Istanbul, Third Preliminary Report*; D. Talbot Rice, *Art of Byzantium*, p. 328, pls. XXIII, 164-5.

103A, B THE MOTHER OF GOD. Mosaic in the apse of the *Cathedral at Torcello*. Mid twelfth century. Unquestionably by a Byzantine artist working in Venetia. (Photos: Alinari.)

Lit: M. Brunetti, S. Bettini, F. Forlati and G. Fiocco, *Torcello*, 1940; O. Demus, 'Studies among the Torcello mosaics', *Burlington Magazine*, LXXXII-LXXXIII, 1943, pp. 136 ff, LXXXIV-LXXXV, 1944, pp. 41 ff, 195 ff; A. Grabar, *Byzantine Painting*, pp. 119-21.

104A, B THE LAST JUDGEMENT. Mosaic on the west wall of the *Cathedral of Torcello*. Mid twelfth century. (Photos: Alinari.) The upper parts seem to be by a Byzantine artist, the lower parts by Venetians. The whole has been not very well restored.

Lit: See 103 above.

105. MANTLE OF KING ROGER II OF SICILY. Silk. *Vienna, Kunsthistorisches Museum.* (Photo: Museum.) An inscription in Arabic states that it was made in the royal workshops at Palermo and dates it 1133-4.

106. KOIMISIS (DEATH OF THE MOTHER OF GOD). Mosaic panel on the west vault of the *Church of the Martorana (Saint Mary of the Admiral), Palermo. c.* 1148. (Photo: Alinari.)

Lit: O. Demus, *The Mosaics of Norman Sicily*, 1949, pp. 73-85, 396-9, pl. 57.

107. PANTOCRATOR. Mosaic in the apse of the *Cathedral at Cefalù*. 1148. (Photo: Anderson.)

Lit: O. Demus, *Mosaics of Norman Sicily*, pp. 3-18, 375-96, pl. 1; A. Grabar, *Byzantine Painting*, 126-8.

108. CAPPELLA PALATINA, *Palermo*. General view of interior, looking east, 1143-54, replanned 1150-70. (Photo: A. F. Kersting.)

Lit: O. Demus, *Mosaics of Norman Sicily*, pp. 25-72, pl. 8.

109. CREATION OF THE BIRDS AND FISHES. Mosaic on the south wall of the *Cathedral at Monreale. c.* 1185. The artists were probably Sicilians trained by Greeks. (Photo: Anderson.)

Lit: O. Demus, *Mosaics of Norman Sicily*, pp. 91-148, pl. 94b. For the architecture of the Norman Sicilian churches see R. Krautheimer, *Early Christian and Byzantine Architecture*, pp. 285-6.

110. SAINT GEORGE. Fresco in the church of *Saint George at Staraya Ladoga, near Novgorod. c.* 1167. (Photo supplied by Professor V. N. Lazarev.)

Lit: V. N. Lazarev, *Old Russian Murals and Mosaics*, 1966, pp. 107-14, pl. 84.

1. UNKNOWN SAINT. Fresco from the *Church of the Annunciation, Arkazhy, near Novgorod. c.* 1189. (Photo supplied by Professor V. N. Lazarev.)

Lit: V. N. Lazarev, *Old Russian Murals and Mosaics*, pp. 114-16, pl. 92.

112. THE LAST JUDGEMENT. Detail from fresco in the *Cathedral of Saint Demetrius, Vladimir. c.* 1195. (Photo supplied by Professor V. N. Lazarev.)
Lit: V. N. Lazarev, *Old Russian Murals and Mosaics*, pp. 81-7, pl. 60.

113. THE TRANSFIGURATION. Detail from fresco in the *Church of Saint Panteleimon at Nerez, in Serbian Macedonia*, founded in 1164 by an Imperial prince, Alexius Comnenus. (Photo: Josephine Powell.)
Lit: P. Muratov, *La Peinture Byzantine*, 1928, pp. 121-3; D. Talbot Rice, *Byzantine Painting*, 1948, pp. 12-13; A. Grabar, *Byzantine Painting*, pp. 141-3.

114. PANTOCRATOR. Miniature mosaic. *Florence, Museo Nazionale*. Mid twelfth century. (Photo: Hirmer.) 'The nearest parallel to the Pantocrator mosaic in the apse at Cefalù' (O. Demus, op. cit., p. 393).
Lit: D. Talbot Rice, *Byzantine Painting*, p. 329, pl. 169; J. Beckwith, *Art of Constantinople*, p. 183.

115. CRUCIFIXION. Miniature mosaic. *Berlin East, Staatliche Museen*. Twelfth century. (Photo: Hirmer.)
Lit: D. Talbot Rice, *Art of Byzantium*, p. 331; J. Beckwith, *Art of Constantinople*, pp. 134-5, dating it late thirteenth century.

116. OUR LADY OF VLADIMIR. Panel painting. *Moscow, Tretiakov Gallery. c.* 1130. The icon was taken from Constantinople to Kiev, probably in 1131, and was moved to Vladimir in 1155. The Virgin is of the type known as 'Eleousa', or 'Our Lady of Compassion'. It has been painted over many times.
Lit: D. Talbot Rice, *Art of Byzantium*, p. 330, pl. 171; A. Banck, *Byzantine Art in the Collections in the USSR*, Nos. 223-4; J. Beckwith, *Early Christian and Byzantine Art*, pp. 131, 183.

117. SAINT JOHN THE BAPTIST, WITH SAINTS PHILIP, STEPHEN, ANDREW AND THOMAS. Ivory relief. *London, Victoria and Albert Museum*. Late eleventh or twelfth century. (Photo: Museum.)
Lit: A. Goldschmidt and K. Weitzmann, *Byzantinische Elfenbeinskulpturen*, II, No. 68; D. Talbot Rice, *Art of Byzantium*, pp. 323-4, pl. 145; J. Beckwith, *Early Christian and Byzantine Art*, pp. 117-18.

118. CHURCH OF THE HOLY APOSTLES. Miniature from the Homilies of James of Kokkinobaphos. *Paris, Bibliothèque Nationale*, Gr. 1208. Early twelfth century. (Photo: Library.)
Lit: *Byzance et la France Médiévale*, No. 36: A. Grabar, *Byzantine Painting*, pp. 180-82.

119. THE ENTRY INTO JERUSALEM. Enamelled silver-gilt plaque from the Pala d'Oro. *Saint Mark's, Venice*. Twelfth century. (Photo: Böhm.)
Lit: See 96 above.

120. TSAR CONSTANTINE ASEN OF BULGARIA. Fresco in the church at *Boiana*. 1259.
Lit: A. Grabar, *La Peinture Réligieuse en Bulgarie*, 1928, pp. 117-76; P. Schweinfurth, *Die Fresken von Bojana*, 1965. (Photo supplied by the Bulgarian Institute of Archaeology.)

121. KING VLADISLAV I OF SERBIA. Fresco in the *Church of the Ascension at Mileševa. c.* 1235.
Lit: S. Radojčić, *Mileševa*, 1963; A. Grabar, *Byzantine Painting*, pp. 143-51; J. Beckwith, *Early Christian and Byzantine Art*, p. 136, pl. 253.

122. KOIMISIS. Detail of group of Apostles from fresco from the *Church of the Holy Trinity at Sopoćani. c.* 1265. (Photo: Josephine Powell.)
Lit: V. Djuric, *Sopoćani*, 1963; A. Grabar, *Byzantine Painting*, p. 151; J. Beckwith, *Early Christian and Byzantine Art*, pp. 136-7.

123. ABRAHAM AND THE ANGELS AT MAMRE (OR THE OLD TESTAMENT TRINITY). Panel painting attributed to Andrei Rublev. *Moscow, Tretiakov Gallery. c.* 1410.

(Photo: Gallery.) Mathew suggests that it was in fact painted in *Constantinople* in about 1400.

Lit: V. N. Lazarev, 'Andrei Rublev and his School' (in Russian), in *History of Russian Art*, published by the Academy of Sciences of the USSR, vol. III, 1955, pp. 102-86; G. Mathew, *Byzantine Aesthetics*, p. 39.

124. SAINT JOHN THE EVANGELIST. Miniature from Gospel. *Paris, Bibliothèque Nationale*, Gr. 54. *c.* 1250. (Photo: Library.) The text is in Greek but with a Latin translation and was clearly made for a Frankish patron.

Lit: K. Wietzmann, 'Constantinopolitan Book-illumination in the period of the Latin Conquest', *Gazette des Beaux Arts*, XXV, 1944, pp. 196 ff; J. Beckwith, *Early Christian and Byzantine Art*, p. 141, pl. 263.

125. CHURCH OF THE PAREGORITISSA, *Arta*. Exterior view. Built 1282-9. (Photo: Josephine Powell.)

Lit: A. K. Orlandos, *The Paregoritissa of Arta* (in Greek), 1963; R. Krautheimer, *Early Christian and Byzantine Architecture*, pp. 294-6.

126A. JACOB AND THE ANGEL. Fresco on the north wall of the north porch of *Saint Sophia, Trebizond*. *c.* 1260. (Photo: Mr Gasilov, Leningrad.)

Lit: Talbot Rice (ed.), *The Church of Saint Sophia at Trebizond*, 1968.

126B. ANNUNCIATION. Fresco, central view of narthex. *Saint Sophia, Trebizond*. *c.* 1250. (Photo: Editions d'Art Albert Skira, Geneva.)

127. THE PROPHET ELIJAH. Fresco in the church at *Gračanica*. 1321. (Photo: Josephine Powell.) The frescoes at Gračanica are signed by the artists Michael and Eutychios, who had previously worked in other Serbian churches.

Lit: H. Hallensleben, *Die Malerschule des Konigs Milutin*, 1965; A. Grabar, *Byzantine Painting*, pp. 151-2; J. Beckwith, *Early Christian and Byzantine Art*, p. 149.

128. THE CHURCH AT GRAČANICA. Exterior view. 1321. (Photo: Josephine Powell.)

Lit: R. Krautheimer, *Early Christian and Byzantine Architecture*, pp. 302-3, pls. 185b, 186a.

129. THE GRAND LOGOTHETE THEODORE METOCHITES. Mosaic in the *Church of Christ in Chora (Kahriye Cami), Constantinople*. (Photo: Byzantine Institute Inc.) Metochites was responsible for the reconstruction and decoration of the church, probably between the years 1315 and 1321.

Lit: P. Underwood, *The Kariye Djami*, 3 vols., 1967 (a full and detailed account, with illustrations of all the mosaics and frescoes). See also G. Mathew, *Byzantine Aesthetics*, pp. 141-3.

130. THE NATIVITY. Mosaic in the *Church of Christ in Chora (Kahriye Cami), Constantinople*. (Photo: Byzantine Institute Inc.)

131. THE PARECCLESION of the *Church of Christ in Chora (Kahriye Cami), Constantinople*. (Photo: Byzantine Institute Inc.) This was added as a funerary chapel and decorated entirely in frescoes, probably in 1320-21.

132. Detail from 131 above.

133. THE ANASTASIS. Detail from fresco in the apse of the Parecclesion, *Church of Christ in Chora (Kahriye Cami), Constantinople*. (Photo: Hirmer.)

134. SAINT EUDOCIA. Incrustation work set in marble. *Istanbul, Archaeological Museum*. (Photo: Hirmer.) The plaque was discovered in the monastery church of Constantine Lips (the Fenari Isa Cami), and has therefore been dated, like the church, to the tenth century, but a later date seems possible. It is the only surviving example of this technique.

Lit: A. Grabar, *Sculptures Byzantines*, pp. 109-10; *Byzantine Art an European Art*, No. 24; D. Talbot Rice, *Art of Byzantium*, p. 325, pl. 149.

135. TWO-MASTED SHIP. Painted on plate. Found during excavations at Corinth. *Corinth Museum*. Thirteenth century. (Photo: Hirmer.)
Lit: *Byzantine Art, an European Art*, No. 667.

136. THE TRANSFIGURATION. Miniature mosaic. Constantinople. Late thirteenth or early fourteenth century. *Paris, Musée du Louvre*. (Photo: Giraudon.)
Lit: J. Beckwith, *Early Christian and Byzantine Art*, p. 145.

137. THE KISS OF JUDAS. Fresco in the *Church of Saint Clement* (originally known as the Church of the Peribleptos) at *Ohrid*. 1295. (Photo: Josephine Powell.) The church was founded by the Greek governor of the city, and the artists who signed the frescoes were Michael and Eutychios, who later worked at Gračanica.
Lit: A. Xyngopoulos, *Thessalonique et la Peinture Macédonienne*, 1955, pp. 34 ff; P. Miljković-Pepek, *L'Oeuvre des peintres Michael et Eutych* (in Serbian and French), 1967.

138. SAINT MERKURIOS. Fresco in the *Church of Saint Clement, Ohrid*. 1295. (Photo: Josephine Powell.)

139. THE CRUCIFIXION, WITH SCENES FROM THE PASSION. Wooden cover of a reliquary containing a fragment of the True Cross. *Venice, Gallerie dell' Accademia*. (Photo: Böhm.) The reliquary itself, of enamel and silver gilt, can be dated by an inscription to *c*. 1300. The cover seems to be about a century later in date. The reliquary was in the possession of Cardinal Bessarion.
Lit: S. Moschini Marconi, *Gallerie dell' Accademia de Venezia, Opere d'arte dei secoli XIV e XV*, 1955, pp. 191-4; A. Frolow, *La Relique de la Vraie Croix*, pp. 563-5; *Byzantine Art, an European Art*, No. 187.

140. THE EMPEROR JOHN VI CANTACUZENUS AS A MONK. Detail from a miniature in the Theological Works of John Cantacuzenus. *Paris, Bibliothèque Nationale*, Gr. 1242. *c*. 1370. (Photo: Hirmer.)
Lit: *Byzance et la France Médiévale*, No. 50; A. Grabar, *Byzantine Painting*, pp. 182-4; D. Talbot Rice, *Art of Byzantium*, pp. 336-7, pls. XXXIX, 190; J. Beckwith, *Art of Constantinople*, pp. 149-51.

141. SAINTS PETER, JAMES AND JOHN. Detail from a miniature of the Transfiguration in the Theological Works of John Cantacuzenus. (Photo: Hirmer.)

142. HUNTING SCENES. Miniatures from the *Cynegetica* of Oppian. *Paris, Bibliothèque Nationale*, Gr. 2736. (Photo: Library.) See 94 above.
Lit: *Byzance et la France Médiévale*, No. 89.

143. BIRTH OF A MONSTER. Miniature from a manuscript of *The Romance of Alexander the Great* (mid fourteenth century, probably executed in Crete). *Venice, the Hellenic Institute of Byzantine and Post-Byzantine Studies*. (Photo: Alinari.) A Turkish translation has been added later to the pages. The monster is a portent foretelling the death of the king.
Lit: A. Xyngopoulos, *Les Miniatures du Roman d'Alexandre le Grand dans le Codex de l'Institut Hellénique de Venise* (in Greek and French), 1966.

144. THE BRONTOCHEION, *Mistra*. Exterior view. *c*. 1300. (Photo: Bildarchiv Marburg.)
Lit: R. Krautheimer, *Early Christian and Byzantine Architecture*, pp. 294 ff.

145. THE MOTHER OF GOD. Fresco in the apse of the *Church of the Peribleptos, Mistra*. Late fourteenth century. (Photo: Josephine Powell.)
Lit: G. Millet, *Monuments Byzantins de Mistra*, 1910, No. 111; G. Mathew, *Byzantine Aesthetics*, p. 155.

146. THE RAISING OF LAZARUS. Fresco from the *Church of the Pantanassa, Mistra*. 1428. (Photo: Josephine Powell.)
Lit: G. Millet, *Monuments Byzantins de Mistra*, No. 140; G. Mathew, *Byzantine Aesthetics*, pp. 155-6.

147A, B. CHURCH OF THE ANNUNCIATION AT VATRA MOLDOVITSA, *Moldavia*. Views of exterior. 1532. (Photos: Monuments Historiques, Bucarest.) The sixteenth-century churches of northern Moldavia, with the exteriors as well as the interiors frescoed in the Byzantine style, form the last important school of post-Byzantine art.

Lit: P. Henry, *Les Eglises de la Moldavie du Nord*, 1930, esp. pp. 179 ff, 228 ff.

148. DIONYSIOU MONASTERY, *Mount Athos*. Paintings in the refectory. Sixteenth century.

Lit: G. Millet, *Le Mont Athos*, 1927, I, pp. 166-8; P. Huber, *Athos*, 1969, pp. 109-11.

149. THE CHURCH OF RISPOLOZHENIA, *The Kremlin, Moscow*. Fifteenth century onwards. (Photo: Novosti Press Agency.)

Books for Further Reading

Of recent years a large number of books on Byzantine art have been published, most of them splendidly illustrated. The most useful general surveys, apart from the thorough but now out-of-date works by C. Diehl, *Manuel d'art byzantin* (2 vols., 2nd edition, Paris, 1925-6), O. M. Dalton's *Byzantine Art and Archaeology* (Oxford, 1911) and *East Christian Art* (Oxford, 1925), and O. Wulff, *Altchristliche und byzantinische Kunst* (2 vols., Berlin, 1916-18), are D. Talbot Rice, *The Art of Byzantium* (London, 1959) and J. Beckwith, *The Art of Constantinople* (London, 1961) and *Early Christian and Byzantine Art* (Harmondsworth, 1970). On architecture there is a comprehensive work by R. Krautheimer, *Early Christian and Byzantine Architecture* (Harmondsworth, 1965). The Early Christian period is covered specifically by M. Gough, *The Early Christians* (London, 1961), W. F. Volbach, *Early Christian Art*, trans. Ligota (New York, 1962), and F. Van der Meer, *Early Christian Art* (London, 1967).

For Byzantine pictorial art, mosaics, frescoes and miniatures, the most useful studies to supplement the general works cited above are S. Bettini, *La Pittura bizantina* (Florence, 1938), A. Grabar, *Byzantine Painting* (London and Geneva, 1953), O. Demus, *Byzantine Mosaic Decoration* (London, 1948), D. Talbot Rice, *Byzantine Painting: the Last Phase* (London, 1968), J. Ebersolt, *La Miniature byzantine* (Paris, 1926), O. Pächt, *Byzantine Illumination* (Oxford, 1952), and the various studies by K. Weitzmann, in particular his *Die byzantinische Buchmalerei des 9. und 10. Jahrhunderts* (Berlin, 1935), and *Illustration in Roll and Codex* (Princeton, 1947).

Provincial schools of pictorial art are covered by G. de Jerphanion, *Les Églises rupestres de Cappadoce* (2 vols., Paris, 1925-42), supplemented by N. and M. Thierry, *Nouvelles églises rupestres de Cappadoce* (Paris, 1963), and M. Restle, *Byzantine Wall Painting in Asia Minor*, trans. Gibbons (3 vols., Recklinghausen, 1967); J. Wilpert, *Die romischen Mosaiken und Materien der kirchlichen Bauten vom IV bis XIII Jahrhundert* (4 vols., Freiburg, 1917) and W. Oakeshott, *The Mosaics of Rome* (London, 1967); G. Bovini, *Ravenna Mosaics* (New York, 1956); E. Diez and O. Demus, *Byzantine Mosaics in Greece* (Cambridge, Mass., 1931); O. Demus, *The Mosaics of Norman Sicily* (London, 1949); A. Grabar and M. Chatzidakis, *Greece. Byzantine Mosaics* (Unesco, 1959); A. Grabar and K. Mijatev, *Bulgaria. Medieval Wall-paintings* (Unesco, 1962); D. Talbot Rice and S. Radojčić, *Yugoslavia. Medieval Frescoes* (Unesco, 1955); A. Banck, *Byzantine Art in Russian Collections* (Moscow, 1965); and V. Lazarev, *Old Russian Murals and Mosaics*, trans. Roniger (London, 1966).

The most important works on individual monuments are, for Saint Sophia E. H. Swift, *Haghia Sophia* (New York, 1940), and for its mosaics T. Whittemore, *The Mosaics of St. Sophia at Istanbul* (4 vols., Oxford, 1933-52), and subsequent articles by P. Underwood and others in *Dumbarton Oaks Papers*, XIV and XV (1960-61). R. Van Nice is preparing a complete structural survey of the building. For the Imperial Palace there is *The Great Palace of the Byzantine Emperors*, 2nd Report, ed. D. Talbot Rice (Edinburgh, 1958). A. Van Millingen, *Byzantine Churches in Constantinople* (London, 1912), is still useful. For the Church of the Chora the three volumes by P. A. Underwood, *The Kariye Djami* (New York, 1966), are essential. Other valuable works are O. Demus, *The Church of San Marco in Venice* (Cambridge, Mass., 1960), and *The Church of Haghia Sophia at Trebizond*, ed. D. Talbot Rice (Edinburgh, 1968). For the monuments at Mistra, G. Millet, *Monuments byzantins à Mistra* (Paris, 1910) is now supplemented by M. Chadzidakis, *Mystras* (in Greek, Athens, 1956).

For the so-called 'minor arts', and for sculpture, important works are A. Grabar, *Sculpture byzantines de Constantinople, 4e-10e siècle* (Paris, 1963), L. Bréhier, *La Sculpture et les arts mineurs byzantins* (Paris, 1936), J. Ebersolt, *Les arts somptuaires de Byzance* (Paris, 1923), N. Kondakov, *Histoire et monuments des émaux byzantins* (Frankfort, 1892), K. Wessel, *Byzantine Enamels*, trans. Gibbons (Shannon, 1969), G. Millet, *Broderies réligieuses de style byzantin* (2 vols., Paris, 1938, 1947), D. Talbot Rice, *Byzantine Glaze Pottery* (Oxford, 1930), and, for numismatics, J. Sabatier, *Description générale des monnaies byzantines* (2 vols., Paris and London, 1862), W. Wroth, *Catalogue of the Imperial Byzantine Coins in the British Museum* (2 vols., London, 1908), H. Longuet, *Introduction à la numismatique byzantine* (London, 1961), and G. Schlumberger, *Sigillographie de l'empire byzantin* (Paris, 1884).

For music and the liturgy useful works are H. J. Tillyard, *Byzantine Music and Hymnography* (London, 1923) and E. Wellesz, *History of Byzantine Music and Hymnography*, 2nd edition (Oxford, 1961), which has an invaluable bibliography, as well as S. Salaville, *An Introduction to the Study of Eastern Liturgies* (London, 1932), G. Dix, *The Shape of the Liturgy* (London, 1943) and V. Cottas, *Le Théâtre à Byzance* (Paris, 1931).

Essential works for the study of the symbolism and meaning of Byzantine art are G. Mathew, *Byzantine Aesthetics* (London, 1963), A. Grabar, *L'Empereur dans l'art byzantin* (Paris, 1936) and *Christian Iconography* (London, 1969), A. Frolow, *La Rélique de la Vraie Croix* (Paris, 1961), K. Weitzmann, *Greek Mythology in Byzantine Art* (Princeton, 1951).

The following Byzantine writers provide descriptions and interpretations of their art: Procopius, *Buildings*, ed. and trans. H. B. Dewing and G. Downey, Loeb edition (London, 1959); Paulus Silentarius, *Descriptio Sanctae Sophiae*, in Migne, *Patrologia Graeco-Latina*, vol. LXXVI, 2; Nicephorus Patriarcha, *Antirrhetici*, in Migne, op. cit., vol. C, and *Refutatio et Eversio*, which is un-published, but relevant extracts are given in P. J. Alexander, *The Patriarch Nicephorus of Constantinople* (Oxford, 1958); *Patria Constantinopoleos*, in *Scriptores Originum Constantinopolitanorum*, ed. T. Preger (Leipzig, 1907); Constantine Porphyrogenitus, *De Ceremoniis*, ed. A. Vogt (2 vols., Paris, 1935-40); Nikolaos Mesarites, *Description of the Church of the Holy Apostles at Constantinople*, ed. and trans. G. Downey, American Philosophical Society, N.S., XLIV, 6 (Phila-delphia, 1957). Photius, *Homily X*, in *The Homilies of Photius*, ed. R. Jenkins and C. Mango (Cambridge, Mass., 1958) describes Saint Mary of the Pharos, not the Nea Basilica, as used to be supposed. There are descriptions of Byzantine buildings by travellers from the West and from Russia: for which see S. Runciman, 'Byzantine Art and Western Medieval Taste', in *Byzantine Art an European Art, Lectures* (Athens, 1966) and B. de Khitrowo, *Itinéraires russes en Orient* (Geneva, 1889). There are many references to Byzantine buildings and works of art in epigrams in the Greek Anthology and in contemporary Byzantine historians, some of which have been collected in J. P. Richter, *Quellen der byzantinischen Kunstgeschichte* (Vienna, 1897). Of medieval Western works, Theophanes, *De Diversis Artibus*, ed. and trans. C. R. Dodwell (London, 1961) describes certain Byzantine techniques. The *Painter's Guide* of Dionysius of Fourna, ed. A. Papadopoulos-Kerameus (St Petersburg, 1900), which used to be thought to represent the eternal canons of Byzantine art, is an eighteenth-century compilation.

Finally, for the best general works on the Byzantine Empire and its civilization, see *Cambridge Medieval History*, vol. IV, new edition (2 vols., Cambridge, 1966-7), A. A. Vasiliev, *History of the Byzantine Empire* (Madison, 1958), G. Ostrogorsky, *History of the Byzantine State*, 2nd edition, trans. J. M. Hussey (Oxford, 1968), *Byzantium*, ed. N. H. Baynes and H. Moss (Oxford, 1938), L. Bréhier, *Le Monde byzantin* (3 vols., Paris, 1947-50), N. H. Baynes, *The Byzantine Empire* (London, 1925), S. Runciman, *Byzantine Civilisation* (London, 1933), J. M. Hussey, *The Byzantine World* (London, 1957), and H. W. Haussig, *A History of Byzantine Civilization*, trans. J. M. Hussey (London, 1971).

Index

FOR THE BEST IN PAPERBACKS, LOOK FOR THE

In every corner of the world, on every subject under the sun, Penguin represents quality and variety – the very best in publishing today.

For complete information about books available from Penguin – including Puffins, Penguin Classics and Arkana – and how to order them, write to us at the appropriate address below. Please note that for copyright reasons the selection of books varies from country to country.

In the United Kingdom: Please write to *Dept JC, Penguin Books Ltd, FREEPOST, West Drayton, Middlesex, UB7 0BR.*

If you have any difficulty in obtaining a title, please send your order with the correct money, plus ten per cent for postage and packaging, to *PO Box No 11, West Drayton, Middlesex*

In the United States: Please write to *Dept BA, Penguin, 299 Murray Hill Parkway, East Rutherford, New Jersey 07073*

In Canada: Please write to *Penguin Books Canada Ltd, 2801 John Street, Markham, Ontario L3R 1B4*

In Australia: Please write to the *Marketing Department, Penguin Books Australia Ltd, P.O. Box 257, Ringwood, Victoria 3134*

In New Zealand: Please write to the *Marketing Department, Penguin Books (NZ) Ltd, Private Bag, Takapuna, Auckland 9*

In India: Please write to *Penguin Overseas Ltd, 706 Eros Apartments, 56 Nehru Place, New Delhi, 110019*

In the Netherlands: Please write to *Penguin Books Netherlands B.V., Postbus 3507, NL–1001 AH, Amsterdam*

In West Germany: Please write to *Penguin Books Ltd, Friedrichstrasse 10–12, D–6000 Frankfurt/Main 1*

In Spain: Please write to *Alhambra Longman S.A., Fernandez de la Hoz 9, E–28010 Madrid*

In Italy: Please write to *Penguin Italia s.r.l., Via Como 4, I-20096 Pioltello (Milano)*

In France: Please write to *Penguin France S.A., 17 rue Lejeune, F-31000 Toulouse*

In Japan: Please write to *Longman Penguin Japan Co Ltd, Yamaguchi Building, 2–12–9 Kanda Jimbocho, Chiyoda-Ku, Tokyo 101*

BY THE SAME AUTHOR

A History of the Crusades

'Whether we regard the Crusades as the most romantic of Christian adventures, or as the last of the barbarian invasions, they form a central fact in medieval history. Before their inception the centre of our civilization was placed in Byzantium and in the lands of the Arab caliphate. Before they faded out the hegemony in civilization had passed to Western Europe. Out of this transformation Modern History was born . . .'

In chronicling this transformation Sir Steven Runciman has written a book which, from beginning to end, enthrals the layman as completely as it satisfies the historian. The excitement of battle, the horror of senseless massacre, the interplay of personalities and ambitions, the effect on the whole development of European history – these are his themes. As he rightly states: 'The whole tale is one of faith and folly, courage and greed, hope and disillusion.'

Volume 1: The First Crusade and the Foundation of the Kingdom of Jerusalem
Volume 2: The Kingdom of Jerusalem and the Frankish East 1100–1187
Volume 3: The Kingdom of Acre and the Later Crusades